Die
Live
Love

James J. Slattery

Published by Pine Creek Press - Dayna Winters, Editor -
a division of Slate Run Publishing, LLC.
www.slaterunpublishing.com

Cover design : Fiona Slattery
Cover photo : Pamela Slattery
Cover painting : Bartolome Esteban Murillo

ROSE, THE (from "The Rose")
Words and Music by AMANDA McBROOM
©1977(Renewed) WARNER-TAMERLINE PUBLISHING CORP. and THIRD
STORY MUSIC INC.
All Rights Administered by WARNER-TAMERLINE PUBLISHING CORP
All Rights Reserved
Used by Permission of ALFRED MUSIC

ISBN: 0692265376
ISBN-13:978-0692265376

DEDICATION

To the three people most responsible for who I am: My mother, my father, and my Aunt Maude (Alla) Nichols. To the one person without whom I would find life intolerable and without whom Love would not have entered my life: My wife, Pamela. To the friend who every day of our very tumultuous history has remained true and who has taught me the meaning of friendship: George Drew.

I love you.

DIE LIVE LOVE

Sojourner, do not lose sight of your baggage
To go lightly is to lose your root

Ghost Stories

"JIM," MY MOTHER cried to my father as she attempted to rouse him from sleep. "There's been an accident, and the young man is dead."

Later, as each recounted the experience, certain inconsistencies were bound to develop, especially in a family such as ours dedicated to the proposition that one should never allow the truth to ruin a good story. Certain elements, however, did remain constant in each of their tellings.

Approximately 1:00 a.m on an autumn night there was an automobile accident, and a young man was in fact killed almost instantly. My father's version from that point on was that the sound of the crash—the car had run off the road and into a tree directly across from our house and their bedroom window—had awakened my mother and that her imagination simply took over from there.

My mother's recounting only incidentally resembled my father's. She had been awakened, not by the sound of the crash, but rather, by the passage of the young man's spirit through the room, brushing her cheek as it went and filling her soul with deep sorrow and a sense of loss. The spirit was alone yet propelled by something off to somewhere it feared to go. The young man cried for her prayers, his voice clear in her mind even as his life-force passed beyond her recognition. Pray for him she did, and in her own mind, succeeded in calming and reassuring the newly—to use her word—"reborn" soul. She would swear until her own dying day that her story happened exactly as she told it, and that she had always been able to "feel" the newly liberated spirits of those who died in her presence or even near at hand.

The year was 1948 and we lived in a house once the headquarters of a black market operation during World War II. Across an expanse of lawn lurked a barn once used as a slaughterhouse. As a seven year old, I played in and around that scene of a thousand deaths. I played as well beneath a flag pole, home to countless snakes, and grew to intertwine in my own imagination the shrieks and bellows of the doomed cattle with the Edenic presence of the reptiles. Added to this, my mother's ghost story instilled in me a sense of the supernatural I found disturbing but not in the least bit frightening.

THREE YEARS LATER, on the sixth of February, 1951, my mother and youngest brother were traveling to Point Pleasant, New Jersey where her brother-in-law, our uncle, had his dental practice. She was to have extensive oral surgery ultimately resulting in upper and lower dentures. The first leg of the journey—we then lived in northern Pennsylvania—was across the southern tier of New York on the Erie Railroad. Once in Jersey City they were to board a train south to Bay Head where my uncle would meet them and take them to his home in Point Pleasant. At Exchange Place, as my mother lifted my brother onto the first step of the car and prepared to board, a voice came to her—she claimed—loud and sure: "Do not take this train," it commanded. Never one to ignore the directly stated will of God or perhaps her Guardian Angel, she pulled my brother back to the platform and waited for the next southbound express. Off they went only to be held up by the wreckage of #733 which had jumped the tracks spilling her intended car off a temporary trestle, killing eighty-five passengers.

My aunt called us and conveyed both the situation and her distress. For the remainder of that evening as time drizzled into early the next morning, we grew increasingly more convinced that my mother and brother were dead. The family gathered; I cried; my father grieved. Eventually the sun rose and soon thereafter relief followed. She had been left stranded and uncomfortable for hours with no means of communicating with anyone either in Pennsylvania or New Jersey, but she and my brother were healthy and well. We had all mourned her as dead. Thus was her phone call a miraculous yet clearly understood mystery, a resurrection. That day…and the next…and the next we gave thanks to God for the miracle he had wrought.

If God acting through the persons of Jesus, Saint Peter or any of the other, even later day, Apostles is, as is metaphorically as well as actually asserted by some, truly a fisherman, then he had me hooked. I believed. Oh, my great and loving God. I believed.

ACCORDING TO MY mother I was the perfect son—Boy Scout, Altar Boy, Future Priest—until I turned sixteen. My father taught me to drive when I was twelve; I had practiced upon many miles by my sixteenth birthday. On that day, September 16, 1957, I secured my Learner's Permit. One week later I took and passed my road test and had my driver's license. On that very morning, my mother claimed, I got behind the wheel and drove away from the scouts, the church, and, most of all, the family. Not so. What I became was a free and independent thinker as well as something of a teen-age rebel. Instead of my role models remaining my parents, the parish priest, the Pope in Rome, I chose James Dean, Elvis Presley, and Marlon Brando. In my own mind I became The Wild One.

I did not, however, leave behind my belief in God.

Until, that is, nine months later. In May of 1958 my mother, having suffered for some time from what seemed to be a cold,

7

took a turn for the worse. For three days she drifted further and further away until, delirious and burning up with fever, she began babbling nonsense. My aunt called the doctor. The doctor called the ambulance, and my mother was delivered to the hospital where she almost died of pneumonia. Her recovery took weeks, and she spent much time thinking and praying. Eventually she summoned us into her room. When we all were gathered, she related the following:

Her life, she oh so piously informed us, had been preserved by God himself, her certainty the result of a visitation by the Holy Blessed Virgin Mary. As my mother waned delirious in the afternoon shadows of her confining little room, a soft voice had called her name. At first it seemed to be her own mother who had died twelve years prior. Such alone would have been miraculous—in Mother's eyes—but there was more to come. Much more.

"Do not seek to find me," the woman whispered. "Our time to be together again is not yet come. Open instead your eyes and see."

My mother would always swear her eyes had not been closed, but when she attempted the impossible—to unobstruct a vision already unoccluded—she found that she had never before truly seen. The incidentals of her life, her hands, the bulk of her body beneath the heavy blankets, the walls, the ceiling, faded into unfocused images not even important as background. That is not to say she was transported, simply that the substantiality of herself and her surroundings no longer asserted its existence as anything of any significance. There was light. And there were shadows. Within the shadows dwelt a mysterious presence. At first, my mother feared she might be experiencing the moment of her death and had fallen beneath the influence of some darkness threatening the salvation of her immortal soul.

"Fear not," the presence comforted. "I am here to see you through, to restore you to your children, to your life. And I shall be with you always." My mother swore she had been visited and was still watched over by the Virgin Mary. This she stated as fact for us all to accept and honor. From that day forward she was, without an official membership, among the Legion of Mary. And we were expected to believe as well.

With the assistance of my next younger brother, she created a Marian shrine in one bedroom—my brother's and mine—and prayed the rosary every day—except when she wasn't drinking. Well, life-altering events are capable of moving us only so far. In fact, after time her devotion cooled and would have disappeared altogether were it not for the fact that she was prone to recurrences of such experiences, although usually of a less dramatic nature, and these would renew her fervor.

BY MY OWN reckoning that morning was the true first step of my journey to myself, to truth, and away from the childish things I once held so dear. First, however, the journey had to lead directly away from its fated destination. Columbus posited that he must sail west in order to reach the East. In global terms, despite his running straight into North America, his reasoning was sound. Metaphorically such was my situation. Always have I pursued enlightenment; from my first conscious moment, just a bit more than a year old, as I gazed upon my mother's face while she lay sleeping, and when I became aware of the train derailment down the block from our apartment in Elmira, New York, I knew something awaited, something beckoned, possibly in the guise of Catastrophe or, I suppose at the time, the thing could have been a warm bottle of formula or even a cold spoonful of vanilla ice cream. I do not know. I do know, however, that during our brief stay in Hellmira, as the sad little city is sometimes called, an even more influential memory is of a time in a swing at the playground of the local school. My father had strapped me into something wooden, and, as I sat gently rocking, he stepped aside to speak with a man in an identical overcoat to his own, to shake his hand, give him a warm pat on the back, and return to me. Meanwhile, sitting alone, I had flown far away. Some black bird or other had perched beside me for a few moments until another flickered by and called, at which point my bird burped a short note and literally disappeared.

That day something called me too. Until two weeks ago I had no idea what had been spoken to me, no idea that I had been selected somehow for a destiny I might never understand. The following is the story of my eventual understanding despite having for the majority of my years sought knowledge, wisdom, and even transcendence in all the wrong places and off in many wrong directions.

CHAPTER ONE

Death

A warrior considers himself already dead, so there is nothing to lose. The worst has already happened to him; therefore he's clear and calm; judging by him, his acts or his words, one would suspect that he has witnessed everything. [1]

ONE DELICIOUS SUNSET afternoon in early June of 1959, the evening of the eve of my high school graduation, my cousin Michael and I got in my father's year-old Buick and drove away from the world of our classmates most of whom were at the school gym celebrating their upcoming maiden lurch into the mysterious, multidimensional future they assumed awaited us all. Whether off to college, the military or a job, whether destined to stay for a lifetime in our small town of Wellsboro, Pennsylvania or wander far off into fields not yet imagined, all expected at least moderately satisfying recompense for the twelve or thirteen years devoted to, as the Salutatorian the next evening would put it, "preparation for success and for life."

Over the last year or so Time had worked much magic upon us. We had discovered the unsurpassable joys of sex and extreme intoxication. Mike and I had also become addicted to speed of both the four and two wheel kind. No one could catch us. Not even the cops who were loath to even try. For certain they could never achieve that acceleration into the universe of unimaginably possible possibilities which we inhabited and which sheltered us from all mundane restrictions, from all *bourgeois* responsibilities, from all idiotic penalty. From Cops, Teachers, Parents. From God Himself if he even existed.

I'm not sure Mike had ever believed in any god. His mother died when he was twelve, and his father, a Marine Corps veteran of the Pacific campaign, avoided churches and religion, often arguing with my mother about such matters. He must not have spent much time in a foxhole; I would bet he fit the definition of someone who would never be found in such. In fact, to hear him tell it, his job was to keep the beer cold for his brother Marines. According to him, Saipan was simply one great drunken brawl the result of some sort of misunderstanding, and a great time was had by all, at least by the Marines. My father told me differently: my uncle Stephen (Brick) was a combat veteran all right, the proof of which was the very fact that he refused ever to talk about such matters. Over time I came to believe my father. There just may have been an atheist in a foxhole, at least that of my Uncle Brick, who died at the age of fifty-five, unrepentant, of lung cancer, the result of at least three packs of Lucky Strikes per day.

I still harbored, if not faith in or love of God, at least a great fear that somebody or something was up there and he or it would surely get me if I screwed up too badly. And so I still went to church, received the sacraments, and dwelt well into some nights upon the horror awaiting me if I somehow could not abandon, whether accompanied or alone—more often the latter—my obsessive sexual activity. I no longer believed in sin; I did however fear Hell even though in no way could I imagine Satan or any other sort of devil as being anything other than a scary counterpoint to the myth of Santa Claus.

So it was that, fearful of the dire consequences of dying with Mortal Sin on my soul yet completely unfocused upon that or any other aspect of spirituality, mortality or teen-age life itself, I set out with Mike upon the first of many random safaris, not always into the dark heart of Conrad's imagination, but oftentimes, such as this one, into one variation or another of a commonplace Northern Pennsylvania rendezvous with death. The Buick's speedometer stretched across before me, mph marked off from 0 to 120, its orange ribbon gauging our run toward an anticipated escape from some gravity the true nature and force of which we could not recognize let alone understand. Nonetheless, in under two minutes we had left our tire's tracks upon the cooling asphalt of the WCHS driveway and were 80 mph down US 6 toward knowledge forbidden in the curricula of public school systems to this day.

From Nichols Street down to Route 6 and then north toward Stokesdale Junction we sped, never slower than twenty miles per hour over the limit except when accelerating or decelerating for the slow-poke sheep and other law-abiding idiots who constantly obstructed our destiny's arrow. We were free, the windows open, a warm wind ruffling our 50's short hair, tickling our teenage scalp. The world itself moved aside, our tires sang not common and uninspired mechanical songs of friction and worn bearings; rather they shouted secular *hallelujahs*, and somehow, although not for the first time, I associated something I had read, but never studied, in school with a truth inexplicably intuited from the world around. Beware.... Beware, my flashing eyes, my floating hair. Hang your heads, you huddled masses, for I on emptiness have fed and drunk from Nothing's sacred cup.

A classmate, neither at the high school gathering nor with us, who would become an academic success of great magnitude in Mathematics, who skillfully if not passionately played the violin, and who dwelt, even in our little rural school, in a land as far off from the average as was Michael's and mine, characterized most of our classmates as sheep. His family, devout Methodists, were well versed in the Christian Bible, as was Lloyd, the difference being that they believed and their son mocked. Thus was he fond of claiming that any god who preferred sheep to human beings must harbor certain unhealthy sexual proclivities, and with that added tinge of sarcasm did he apply his ovine analogy to humanity in general. Mike and I had come to share his jaded, as he termed it, agnosticism and to embrace his less than generous perception of the common run of humanity. But, while he removed himself into the world of Calculus, imaginary numbers, and beyond, we simply pushed our pedals to the metal and soared off into the great wide open which exists only for young men and women of that certain age and disposition. Lloyd lost his lower nature in the finer things of the mind while we blindly sought to erase them both.

That very day the sheep were herded in minimally spaced clumps over a too long for us to countenance distance, and so it was that we stayed over 80 mph in the left-hand lane for most of a mile and blew past six or seven family sedans filled with foolish children and no-mind adults until the road opened clear ahead. But then.

Bam! A thunderbolt or at least a '57 Olds Rocket 88. We had never seen it before; it was beautiful, black with minimal chrome, and lowered just a bit in the rear. As this unwelcome intruder dipped in beside us, my heart stopped while simultaneously gathering for an adrenaline-fueled plunge into a race I was certain to lose. No way could my old-man's Buick, top of the line as it was, defeat a Rocket 88. But I would not drop behind, and so, as the other driver taunted me by slowing down, I dug my foot into the floorboard, and the race was on. Fifty four years later, the proud Captain of a Dodge Charger Hemi, I childishly enjoy playing with lesser vehicles and their drivers by matching their speed tenth of a mile by tenth of a mile rather than letting them go their ill-conceived ways, then with a jolt of acceleration leaving them hopelessly behind. I believe this propensity was the first of the lessons I learned that day so long ago. Mr. 88 was toying with me. 100, 110, 120, the ribbon buried. He stayed beside us. Never did he turn his bland profile our way. Without effort he simply matched our speed. I was bested. I knew it. I would not back down.

Time did not seem to stop despite the fact that the nearer we approach the speed of light the slower it actually does unfold, and we were 120 mph faster than our at-rest selves having accelerated and flattened out at $1/5,580,000^{th}$ the speed of light above and beyond the normal light-approaching speed of our revolving planet in this our expanding universe. Lloyd would have broken out his slide-rule had he needed it. Mike and I merely accepted the static circumstances of our wooly perceptions. I cannot be certain of his awareness or lack of such at the time, for I only knew one thing: I had lost, and my defeat continued to mock me, side by motionless side with my failing Buick. Never had I tasted such bitterness—yes, hopelessness—before.

Closer and closer ahead of us, facing off southbound in its proper lane, grew another presence, an old junker it turned out. We were on a collision course. The approaching car was in no manner threatening save for the fact that we were headed straight for it at two miles per minute. And what did I care? In fact, I could not have cared less. Something within me opened to a grand and decidedly ultimate possibility. Ahead lay death.

In that instant I knew something perhaps best expressed not in as many words as it now takes to explain, but in a form even more complexly simple than language other than poetry is capable of expressing. Before me dwelt a truth, which throughout the few years of my life had kept itself from me, concealed within Catholic doctrine, the pieties of my mother's visitations, my brothers' reliance upon something somewhere greater than themselves. I saw past the shepherd's merciful obstruction of his lambs' ability to recognize so much more than the mere existence of the wolf which much prefers little pigs, but rather I became aware of the predator's presence always within their trusting midst.

I saw death. Clearly as somehow erotically comforting.

I prepared to embrace my new lover as never had I been able to do one of the two quart women with whom I occasionally experienced at least a hint of an out-of-body reality in the backseat of someone else's old car. At a much later date in an aquarium, perhaps Boston or Coney Island, but I would bet Mystic, Connecticut, I came upon a tank containing a lazily circling shark. I stood before it transfixed; its eye, empty of all, even hate or hunger, spoke to me of the moment so long ago as I faced death in the form of an old car so casually drawing nearer on another warm summer's day. The shark's beauty is unparalleled except by a very few other such manifestations of the spiritual nature of the world as is Blake's Tyger burning ever so bright in the dark forests of our mortal night. Or an old Chevy trailing smoke and greedily consuming June's deceptive sunlight.

My wrist resting easily upon the power steering wheel, my consciousness opened to the cold of the Pennsylvania forest around me, the shimmer of the coming summer's heat upon the blacktop, but, above all, to the emptiness surrounding everything we know or may know. As the hydrogen furnace of biological casting burned itself toward black but a single Astronomical Unit, roughly 92,955,807.273 miles away, the compelling gravity of surrender to a truth greater than any of these rose above its dark horizon, but I did not submit; instead I took not a leap of faith but one of indifference directly into the event so clear and open before me. I would not be upheld, would drop upon no soft cushion. With no hope. No fear. I died.

"Jim... Jim!" my cousin cried. "Do something.... We're going to die."

At the time I had not heard of the neuroscientific explorations chronicling the supposed non-existence of free will as evidenced by the Libet experiment and its subsequent variations, but had I, I might at the moment have found myself agreeing with later-day assumptions that these experiments tend at least to deny the reality of individual autonomy. I had died, but, without thought or any sort of concern, I saved Michael's life. A mere spasm of my wrist and my fender moved into the 88's space; the Rocket slowed, and with no more than inches between the Olds on our right and the Chevrolet to the left, we slid into a perfect space for an orange sunshine Buick to insert its one-hundred-twenty mph bulk.

Life resumed its illusion of normalcy. Mike shook, and I would seem to remember, gasped out several sounds not at all unlike sobs, although in his elaborate and somewhat embellished retellings, he never cried out for his life at the point in time and space where death and I became forever one.

From then on I have had no fear of death, for it is only the end of a small and temporary stage in the evolution of this manifestation of consciousness, spirit, and physicality we call life. For the first time I realized there was something—a deluded something I was certain—to my mother's stories. At the very moment of my end I shall not pass away diffusing into the undetectable mists of nowhere; neither shall I continue to be the old me in some new world or enter into a heaven or hell. True enough, I shall once again, as they say, die, but my dying will simply be another step in my becoming. Once I burst through the thin membrane of the amniotic sac within which we the living dwell, the next evolutionary stage of my eternal life will have been achieved. Physically, the zygote becomes the embryo, the fetus, and eventually, biologically, the human being whose development ends after the stages of infancy, childhood, adulthood, old age, and death. Upon completion of that process, the essential human, the conscious spirit, does not cease to exist, but continues into another stage of its own development. What that is I do not know.

How I know the truth of that which I have just asserted rests upon ground unrecognized by science or perhaps even speculative logic. It is said that the mystical experience is ineffable, that in its reduction to words it is not merely altered but is destroyed. My June moment upon the highway was a mystical experience. I say I died. That is as close as I may come. Eliot's Prufrock, a decidedly unheroic, less than admirable creation, poses a significant question when he asks the lady of his fearful mind whether if he were Lazarus come back from the dead she would even care. His question away from the context of the poem becomes even more profound. I have read several near-death recollections and have found them at best unconvincing, and worse, the uninspired imaginings of someone so steeped in the conventional that should their "heaven" be actual I no doubt would prefer the Greeks' version of Hell. Therefore, I present my own graduation into death with no little trepidation. I am not my mother. But I am her child.

I have died. I have seen nothing. I am not afraid.

The absence of fear is due to something I felt at that moment. I give it no name other than Death. But I also know for certain, beyond even the possibility of doubt or the need for hope, that physical death is not the end. I am, however, unable to give the reader any further glimpse into the circumstances of that estate, but the necessary perceptions are possible, perhaps inevitable for us all. We each shall someday encounter the Shark, the Tyger or face down an old Chevrolet aimed straight for us as an anonymous number 88 holds us true to our appointed end.

Michael

I SIT HALF a century older at a coffee shop table writing this. Michael has been physically dead for most of that time. The year he died was 1978. I do not remember the month or the day, nor do I care to make the call which would give the information to me. In his own way I think he died well before that afternoon prior to graduation and certainly many years before 1978. As a 17-year old innocent I moved ahead blind to the circumstances surrounding me, the situations left behind, the actual possibility of any future beyond perhaps a week's time. Once much later as an English instructor at a community college I had occasion to spend some time with a member of the psychology department who taught some sort of self-help nonsense concerning short-term and long-term goals. I was at least thirty-five, and for the first time I became aware of the fact that many, possibly most, people in some fashion or other, plotted out the course of their lives. As I exclaimed to her when she finally convinced me that such was the case: "Holy shit."

Never have I had nor ever intend to have anything resembling a goal whether long, short or immediate. An expression I believe not yet common in 1959, "Go with the flow," would best express the pattern of my life were it not for the fact that those words themselves imply choice. One either goes along or does not. Either conscious or subconscious choice enters the picture. Better for me is this: On the Pennsylvania highway I came upon a black hole of some as yet undiscovered gravity; I unwittingly drove into its inescapable pull; from then my life simply happened. My thirty-something self felt only gravity. To him there was, could be, nothing more.

Another possibility did unfold itself along my way, but for this time this is Michael's story, and I digress. Some dark star similar to but different from mine held Mike within its horizon, and I am left with questions and no possibility of understanding even if answers should miraculously appear.

Why, Michael, while on summer vacation from Penn State, did you and a friend, recently discharged as undesirable from the Army, drink yourself senseless, break into a beer distributor's business directly across from the main gate of a factory just as one shift was ending and another beginning? Why did you park your readily identifiable 1940 Ford right out front? Why for fifty dollars and four cases of beer did you submit to a felony conviction which easily might have been reduced to a lesser charge?

I REMEMBER THE afternoon of your mother's undoing. My

mother sat us down and in hushed tones explained that Aunt Clara had suffered a stroke while in the dentist's chair. I was twelve and idiotically enough had no idea what a stroke was; neither did my brothers. Explaining as best she could to a huddle of children seemed to lighten my mother's burden, and afterward we all went for Texas hot dogs and soft ice-cream rather than eating at home. My aunt was alive—in the hospital, but alive—and hospitals were places where babies were born and the sick got well. She would recover. We prayed. We trusted. We knew.

Mike and my cousin Stephen, "Pug," hard of hearing and slow of speech, came to stay with us. Mike and I had no fear and went about our lives as though on holiday. Pug's head hung; his appetite, even for banana splits, deserted him. We mocked the tremble in his lip, his increased tendency to mispronounce and misspeak. He was fifteen; my mother brushed back the hair from his forehead and took his hand in hers as she comforted him. Mike and I could not contain our laughter. Three years older, Pug was still the baby.

My uncle stopped in the second night. Drunk. There had been no change in Aunt Clara's condition. Our lives went on.

A FEW BLOCKS away in a seedy commercial part of town we called the Bowery was a combination short-order, ice-cream and soda shop just reopened as "The Teen Club." Those of us who at twelve entertained pretentions of adulthood spent untold hours at the counter drinking coffee every once in a while but soda more often, listening to the latest rock-and-roll on the new jukebox, and playing one of the three pinball machines. Mike and I had for the time a free pass from responsibility, and so it arrived that one school day afternoon, the Teen Club deserted but for us, the news that would rock and roll Michael directly into a place I yet knew not existed. Her soft hand touched my shoulder straining at the flippers. "Where's Mike?" my mother asked. "I have to talk to him." Oh, God I knew.

But not Michael Charles. As he came around the corner from the Men's Room and spied my mother, his eyes brightened and his freckled face lit up with delight. "Hi, Aunt Martie," he beamed, certain, I am sure, that she bore long anticipated good news.

She took him outside to her car to tell him his mother was dead. The details were never fully revealed to me. By my mother's accounting, he simply grew a little paler, remained silent, nodded when she asked if he understood, and simply got out of the car and disappeared back into the Teen Club. If I knew anything then or know anything now, I am certain she attempted with all her heart to smother him with her dark arms of love and compassion, to spread the balm of her kisses across his tearless cheeks and into his aching heart. I am as certain she failed. Michael's heart was beyond aching. His orphaned soul would admit no comfort. That day he turned his face from life.

He returned to the pinball beside mine. And tore it up. Ringing free game after free game from its glass and steel keep. I looked at him but once.

"Is she?" I asked.

Mike simply nodded and clanged up six free ones with one magnetized, misplaced steelie welded to an electric leaking bumper of some red and yellow amalgam. We never spoke of the day. We never mentioned his mother. Ever. She was dead and so was he.

A father already changed by a war he never admitted to fighting, a mother dead of her own internal weakness, my cousin stood abandoned. And he knew it. My mother tried. And failed. As his father adventured with Scotch Whisky and women, among them his best friend's wife, as his brother slipped further and further from immediate contact with any coherent approach to life, Michael was unable to understand, yet came to live the code of the warrior. At least in his own eyes, he was already dead. In that state he regularly succeeded at eating and drinking. Michael

Charles, however, never could be merry.

I look back, having discovered ways to live, perhaps even meaningfully, while acknowledging the fact of my own death, and wonder why Mike spoke that day in the car. The words "We're going to die," must have contained no dread in his consciousness. His words must have been for me. Why did he save me? What did he know?

IN THE SUCCEEDING years I have chanced upon the Calvinist concept of The Elect. I am no Calvinist. I do not believe as doctrine in the principle of unconditional election, nor of human sinfulness and salvation, but in my own way, I do believe in God, and that belief involves none of the aforementioned doctrinal concerns. As well, I consider myself a Christian, a follower of Jesus free of the obfuscation, error, and falsehood inherent in all of the cults now given US Constitutional validity. And I find I am of an elect unrecognized both by Calvin and his theological predecessor Augustine, and that election grants me a life of joy and fulfillment despite my best efforts to avoid such human impossibilities.

That is why Michael spoke up. That is why I draw breath on this day and he does not. For that I thank God. Because of that I am left with the question one such as I must ask, "Why me, Lord?" Kris Kristofferson attempts an answer and asks a question as well, how can he repay all that has been given him? His answer is to show someone else what he has been through. I am no lyricist, so I cannot attempt a reply in kind. The simple truth: No repayment is possible nor is it even desired. Mike's father turned to distractions, possibly due to his own abandonment; my cousin had no loving father available, no entangled consciousness and spirit. I have been given so very much more.

Another question arises however. Was Michael Charles McInroy's life's purpose merely to save mine and aid in the inception of my own unique consciousness; was his influence upon his short-term wife another; was the conception of his two daughters perhaps his true *raison d'etre*? No doubt I will never know. I do, however, firmly hope, despite my belief that hope is an illusion necessary only for the weak of heart and spirit, that his life was somehow for himself and that his small influences upon the lives of others were incidental to a grander purpose of some unknowable nature.

At the time of his death in the ebb and flow of my life there was much more apparent ebb than flow. In fact the ebb had been seriously depleted by the scarcity of any flow of any significant nature. The moon had risen with very little ocean to tug upon and move in any direction whatsoever. Once upon a long time after Michael's passing, as a favor to a very dear friend, a new James of rising tides participated in a Cancer Survivors' twenty-four hour Walkathon. Six of us circled a community college track from the hour of 3:00 am until 4:00. A usually jovial bunch of martial artists, we wound round and round mostly silent. The father of the ill child (Leukemia), our *Sensei* walked with us. In the face of childhood cancer there is nothing worthwhile saying. When the hour was done, the father stayed until dawn; the rest of us, Black Belt Warriors all, deserted the field, T-shirts in hand, grateful for something we truly did not understand.

At a not too much later time, however, the child declared cancer-free, I had occasion to meditate upon the concept of the survivor, of survival itself. We all may survive automobile accidents, dread diseases, war, and pestilence. But we cannot survive life. Michael gave me many more years. Medicine gave the *Sensei's* son renewed good health and the possibility of his own longer time. No one, however, no institution, study, art or science, can make us immortal. This awareness is, of course, so common as to be a cliché, but, as with much that is trite and unexceptional, it is inescapably true. And so, directly relevant to my ego-centric self, the questions arose. Why? Who cares? Do I? At that moment I could not even begin to adequately answer the first of these. And the only answer to the second was, "I hope my wife, children, immediate family, and friends." But am I certain that they authentically care about my life independent of theirs or is their concern all wound up within personal concepts of well-being and supposed dependence? The answer to the third question, "Yes." Emphatically, "Yes." And that leads directly back in a most frustrating loop to "Why?"

Throughout much of my life from the near-collision afternoon on, I have dwelt within the comfort of Camus' condemned man. For most of that same time, however, I have also taken refuge within the illusion of rather than experiencing the actuality of freedom. Behind the wheel of my father's Buick I saw into the void behind the eyes of the Tyger, and my course was set. But I did not find out its direction or its destination—other than death—until much later when a series of visions and verbal communications *a la* Martha McInroy Slattery (my mother), a shocking and psychically violent wrenching—more profound than any collision ever could have been—stripped bare the actual immortal which I now am.

And so, I find myself something of a survivor, although I cannot help but wonder if ever there is or has been anything it is essential that I survive. A friend once long ago proposed that the evolution of his own unique self, someone Nietzsche might have held as an ideal, substantially resulted from his having found himself within the jaws of the saber-tooth tiger, and his primal response of ripping himself free, a bloody tusk in one fist, the tiger's jaw unhinged, its life's blood heart-beating upon the sand. He is certain a similar event must have happened in my life.

Even though the following questions may be ridiculously naive, I am led to wonder if a beat-up Chevy is in some other reality a sabre-tooth tiger. And did my friend have anyone else there to call him from the jaws? Obviously, the tiger is metaphorical, so too may an automobile be, but that Chevy was real. Michael ripped me from its maw. I did not even consider for the most fleeting of moments doing so myself. On the other hand, my friend has acted in his own behalf even when overmatched by the most horrendous of circumstances; I am alive because of Mike. My survival has never been my own choice.

Does it matter?

CHAPTER TWO

A life most simple? Most ordinary?
"And *therefore* most terrible." [2] (Emphasis mine)

THE QUESTIONS ABOVE in different linguistic clothing open
Section *II* of Leo Tolstoy's *The Death of Ivan Ilych*. At the outset of
my own second stanza I must offer something of an explanation,
possibly more a disclaimer. I wish I were not so completely
indebted to the great yet almost fatally flawed Russian. But I am,
and *Ivan* has assumed an iconic spot in my consciousness, my
spiritual reality, and my heart.

My initial love of Tolstoy, however, sprung not from his
writing, but from the movie *War and Peace* and my adolescent
fixation upon Audrey Hepburn. Our small-town theater, The
Arcadia, usually ran only very limited showings of any movie, but
War and Peace was given a week. I think I saw it five different
times, once sitting from matinee through evening show. By the
final close I had ensconced Audrey within my heart—wherein she
yet dwells—and had become swept up in the grand scope of
everything even tangentially relating to the actual historical
personages of Napoleon, Tsar Alexander, and General Kutuzov.
More so, I developed for possibly the first time a true affection for
fictional characters. Henry Fonda's words, "Damn you Napoleon.
Damn you to Hell." remain alive within my memory to this day. I
see him. I hear him. At the time (15 years old) I questioned
Pierre's turning from one of my favorite romantic—despite his
being a devoted neo-classicist—historical personages. Presently,
the words ring, within a more sympathetic consciousness. Truly,
Damn you, Napoleon, although, despite myself, I still very much

admire you.

I still smile, and my heart beats faster when I remember the young man who after the final Wellsboro showing of *War and Peace* waited around, supposedly assisting Cousin Michael as he changed the Marquee. I do not remember the next film, but I vividly do remember and still mourn the letters as they fell into Mike's careless hands. He had seen the movie several days before and simply experienced the magic as just another in a long line of superficial distractions, pleasurable and forgettable. I grieved silently. He finished, and then we snuck down an alleyway to share a smoke.

At the time books were cheap, and probably because of the movie, paperback copies of the epic were available even in Wellsboro, a town with no bookstore. The next day I snuck two dollars from my mother's pocketbook and bought my ticket into the land of serious literature even though I eventually discovered the chosen book had been abridged and was only about half the original. So, not six months later I did what any young man whose bogus ticket had nonetheless effected his transport to his chosen destination would do; I checked a complete translation—I forget whose—from the town library, and after two renewals, when they would no longer let me keep it, I returned the new scripture of my life until it was once again nestled within its alphabetically correct station. Then I stole it.

AN ESSAY SUCH as this one, the ultimate concern of which is the discovery of God and its attendant metamorphosis, might be forgiven for overlooking the minor indiscretions and immoralities common to most young men and women and, while sin is a necessary presence in tales of redemption as the evil from which one is delivered, mine, such as the minor pilfering and later more grievous transgressions of that morality most commonly recognized as valid by both believer and atheist such as "Thou shalt not steal," are yet with me, and are a substantive component of the God-centered creature I have become. I remember most of them, and will reveal more. For now let it be known that petty, extremely petty, thievery is not foreign to the one writing at this moment in this present tense he perceives as real. For the most part, however, I value honesty and have cost myself substantial gain by doing the right thing, by paying the cost, both monetary and personal, for most of the insignificant peripherals of the life we humans hold so dear.

My primary affliction or perhaps blessing has been an inability to truly care about most of these very trappings of modern American, middle-class life. I love my motorcycle and my car, but, at the same time they are mere adjuncts, pleasurable and temporary, to any authentic self. The same holds for clothing, houses, titles, social or educational achievement. There are many more not worth mentioning. I do, however, value family, love, and that which Van Morrison termed "A sense of wonder." And that sense of wonder which has guided my life since the school-year 1967-1968, surfaced in my consciousness as the direct result of my reading *The Death of Ivan Ilych* for the first time.

A BIT OF background is necessary for a full comprehension of this event. From the very beginning I was my father's protégé and I dare to say favorite. He took me with him to places a child may never even imagine. He had a friend, Mark, something of an Irish gangster who would come to visit on regular and often very tense occasions—my mother disapproved of him and made no secret of her distaste. But, after he left, having sat on our horsehair couch for the entire duration of his visit, my brother and I would mine the crack between seat and back for the change which never failed to fall from his pocket. The time was the late 40's and early 50's. The change always totaled several dollars each, no inconsiderable sum in those days. My mother insisted we donate it to the church.

My father overruled her. We were rich.

That is not the best of it. At times, tiring of Mom's harsh silence, the two men would take me with them into a wonderland of adventure. We went to bars. I drank "pop" alongside the men, and we traveled in the most marvelous of cars. A Packard. Chauffeur-driven. Mark and Pa sat in back. I sat up front with a dark man whose name seemed to be "Cap," who, before we left home or any of our stops, would mount two magnetized Scotch Terriers, one black, the other white, at the front of the extra-long hood, and, as we traveled, the vibrations would move them toward us until they eventually came to rest right up at the windshield.

There was more. Cap carried a pistol. He would let me hold it sometimes as we drove. My mother would have died. Or perhaps killed. My father had other business, the nature of which I never was to know, to occupy his attention. He was not, however, unaware. The man never hunted nor did he seem at all attached to guns of any sort. In fact more than once I heard him speak against those who found some validation of their masculinity in their rifles. However, he did for some time not seem inclined to rid himself of the two pistols he kept, one in his and my mother's bedroom and the other in the little den we called the "sewing room." They did eventually disappear, and good thing. I learned of their absence the result of searching for one with which to threaten and perhaps use upon a bully who had done my little brother a serious wrong. Thank you, God, for my father's eventually having seen the light.

Perhaps as a direct result of my experiences with Mark and Cap as they drove my father and me along the twisted roads of Northern Pennsylvania off into the sweet-scented atmosphere of barrooms, loud and portentous discussion, and the romantic allure of a male universe at a far remove from the safe old house in Wellsboro and its female and child-centered consciousness, I seem forever destined to seek for light in darkness, find stability in motion, and peace only in contention. To this day, as clearly as does the head-on junker, the two Scotties slide along their metal path toward me promising something I still value, yet fail to recognize. The movement of the Packard through the wilderness air, the freedom of a man with a gun, the wholly accepted imprisonment of the man, Mark, in the back seat who was soon to begin a long Federal sentence. It was all of it part of being a man. This much I knew. But I did not even begin to know it all.

Hard upon the occasion of Mark's last visit just prior to his surrender to the authorities, I asked my father if he too might be going to jail. At that his bulldog face broke into one of those completely innocent and loving smiles he seemed so easily capable of projecting even under the most trying of circumstances. "No," he assured me. "Your mother won't let me." For an eleven or twelve-year man-to-be such was promise enough, and he was true to his word. Or to his wife, whichever might have been the case.

MY FATHER MUST somehow have recognized my need for a higher level of education than most fledglings are exposed to. Enter Porky Monroe. Porky was a butcher. He owned a shop. He slaughtered and prepared his own meat. Always seeming happy, ever ready with a joke or some other pithy comment which I couldn't understand, yet which was certain to coax both his famous smile and at the least a small chuckle from my father, Porky who stood perhaps five foot five and seemed at least that big around as well, according to my father was the strongest man he had ever known. Look at his forearms he told me. They're even bigger than your Uncle Jack's.

It was to Porky that my father assigned the role of advanced placement instructor. On Saturdays in the fall my father would stop at an isolated inn, The Twin Pines, in the town of Ansonia, where he would fill a gallon jug with draft beer, and we would then drive up into the forest to a place with parking, picnic tables, and stone grills. All this perched upon the edge of a deep cleft in the howling colors of a northern autumn. At the very bottom ran Pine Creek (*Crick*), along which coursed the tracks of The New York Central Railroad. My father would immerse himself in Notre Dame Football while I built fires, wandered the pine-carpeted trails, and listened for the sound of an approaching train.

When The Fightin' Irish won, our homeward journey would be filled with happy talk, humorous critiques of those at home, those who failed to love Notre Dame, and my mother's entire family except my Uncle Brick. When ND lost, however, the passage would be mostly silent, interrupted now and then by an uncharacteristic curse mumbled from between beer-numb lips. On those days we also refilled the jar at the Pines and the ride back to town would assume an element of not unwelcome danger. Without his intending it, my father's driving taught me a lot about living on the edge. "There is no tomorrow," he would roar above the noise of our travel. "Remember, Jaz, those APA bastards'll take everything you have. They'd steal your soul if they could. Remember," he would snarl, and his eyes would threaten things better left unsaid. "Remember. Trust nobody. Your family's all you've got." Then more often than not he would soften for a brief period, sometimes long enough for us to reach safety. One particular afternoon of Notre Dame defeat, however, he neither drank during nor after the game and made none of his usual negative references to prejudiced officiating and Protestant rapacity. Instead, after the final whistle, we took a new tack. We were off to see Porky Monroe.

IN A NEW direction, a roundabout way along dirt rather than paved highway they travel until arriving at a dilapidated garage-type structure set back maybe fifty feet from the road. Unpainted in the sense of never painted, its rough-cut slab siding blackened in the relentless air of North America. Two red doors meet in the

31

middle of a better-than-car-width portal. They park directly in front. "What are we doing?" asks the unsuspecting child.

"We're meeting Porky," assures the parent.

"Why?" inquires the lad.

"You'll see," comes his father's answer as around to the side they progress and make to enter through a white and stained door. "We'll just be a minute or two," his father assures him. "We have to help Mr. Monroe with something."

In they go.

VISUAL MEMORY OFTEN serves an elusive reality. I harbor no doubt that the ensuing events occurred as I relate them here; the scene has remained immutable in my mind. Still, from where exactly does it originate? Is it as it actually stood in verifiable reality or is it so colored by imagination and emotion as to be misleading, either less gruesome or more so than I now envision? In support of the actual emotional reality of my memory, I experienced no trauma. I never viewed the scene and the events as grisly or even particularly unpleasant until I related them to a friend at least forty years afterward. The man was appalled, and asserted that my father had been abusive in his behavior. I disagree. To this day I believe that in Porky Monroe's backwoods shed I learned a most valuable lesson, one that even the new me treasures, a lesson which fully prepared me to face oncoming death whether by fire, ice or velocitous iron. And one that prepared me to face the truth of *Ivan Ilych*.

Later, my father would laugh and say the smell almost turned us away. I remember no smell. Instead, I see shadow, black, gray, and faded brown. I see twisting forms projected upon white walls. Directly before me flickers no shadow. Front legs held splayed by chains, head cranked low by more chain slipped through a ring imbedded in the floor, stands a cow. My father and I pause before it. Porky fills the place with his absence.

"Where's...?"

"Shhhhh.... He'll be here."

And he is. From behind what now in memory must have been a rawhide curtain emerges Mr. Monroe. At first his great bulk is more shadow than substance, but as he approaches alongside the animal, his incidentals become clear. He is clad in a white shirt, white pants, black rubber boots, and wears a long and spotless white apron tied snugly about his girth. In his right hand he wields a sledgehammer, swinging it lightly and rhythmically as one might a baton. "Jim," he nods to my father. "Son," to me.

"Porky," my father replies.

"You sure about this?"

"Absolutely."

"It's a lesson, son," Porky addresses to someone beyond us all. "One your Daddy thinks you're old enough to learn. You OK?"

THE BOY IS no fool, but he has to ask. "Are you going to kill the cow?"

"It's not a cow," Porky instructs. "It's a yearling bull. Good for nothin' but eatin'."

"How you gonna to do it?" the child asks.

"Shhh," his father cautions.

"It's OK, Jim. Son, as they say, actions speak louder than words."

As Porky turns to the yearling the boy can see recognition in its eyes, hear the beginnings of a blat, but all other sound is crushed by the impact of the butcher's hammer delivered sure and true as truth can ever get to the center of the beast's head. There is no blood.

Monroe stands aside, perhaps unsure of what to do next. The father lays a gentle hand on his son's shoulder, then turns the boy's face up to his and smiles. "That, Jaz, is where our meat comes from. That is how we live. Now, go on out to the car. I'll be with you in a minute."

The boy complies, and to this day prays to the shade become of his father, "Thank you, Pa," for all you have done for me, for all you have given me, for the absolute truth you once taught me.

THE CONNECTION BETWEEN the above events and the soul-wrenching impact of *The Death of Ivan Ilych* appears not at all tenuous to me. As a matter of fact the second of these moments would have been impossible without the first, and the first could not have led anywhere, at least in my personal reality, but to the second. Between the two, much, mostly of a diversionary nature, intervened, and most of that was inimical to the clarity Ivan's last moments would engender within the oppressive walls of my Bourbon and pot-smoke room.

I had a degree in English but had never read the most celebrated of my hero Tolstoy's short stories. I did, however, have a job as an English teacher in a community college; it was my first year, second trimester, and the course outline required teaching the too-long story our anthology rightly classified as a *novella*. The day was Saturday. Monday I was scheduled to begin *Ivan*. I would read first and then search the library for the relevant scholarship.

To this day I teach a course entitled *The Short Story*, and I still teach *Ivan*. By the end of that day, however, I imagined that I could never again lie half stoned and a quarter drunk in a dim little room plotting a routine approach to another piece of someone else's literature, in someone else's employ, and for someone else's benefit. I was reborn into the James J. Slattery I had once been born to be.

For many years, I had been shackled, a thin haze of dimwitted presentiments intermittently arising from out the cowshit mud of my bovine non-understanding. The ever present butcher had stood by my side for more than a decade while I myself gawked blindly before me. But that Sabbath, when the hammer raised by the hairy arm finally began its swift descent, I awoke. Once again, the yearling, skull cracked, sagged in its chains. But as before, I passed on to my father's car, and he drove me home.

IVAN'S LIFE IS presented as being "most simple, most ordinary," and as a result of this tedious if not tragic normalcy, "most terrible." It most certainly was nothing like mine. My father was a man of secrets, a binge-drinking alcoholic, the spoiled favorite of an aunt not his aunt, an unfaithful yet passionate husband. He was bitter, violent, and full of hate for many people, institutions, and attitudes. Never though was his hatred directed at the downtrodden, the hopeless or even such enemies of my youthful America as the Russians. He championed Khrushchev over both Eisenhower and Kennedy. He hated Richard Nixon. Most impressive in my mind is his uncommon sense of the injustices suffered by the oppressed African Americans (Negroes) of his time, fueled primarily I believe by his sense of being descended from another enslaved people, the European Irish. "They did it to everyone," he would rant. "The British."

An incident in St. Petersburg, Florida in 1946 remains with me to this day. Perhaps my Father's shining moment, one of a kind Ivan never could have known. My Maternal Grandmother had died up north in Dolgeville, New York. My mother and my brother John were traveling by bus to her funeral. My Father and I would stay behind for reasons I did not understand. A typical Pinellas day it was, the Sunday of her leaving. They had dressed me for Mass in the Sailor suit I so much hated, and I still wore it as we bade her good-bye. We were early. The bus stood idling, door open, driver smoking to the side. Smartly striding, skin as black as his spit-shined shoes, a Marine, the left sleeve of his dress greens neatly pinned up to the shoulder above his missing arm, approached the vacant transport. As the warrior reached for the chrome handrail the paunchy driver snarled. "Hold on, Nigger. You wait 'till the white folk board."

I was not yet five, but I remember clearly the sudden gravity of my Father's reaction. The crimson flaming above his starched collar. I can hear my mother's alarmed caution. I will never forget the scene my Father made. No man to waste words, short and mean as a Jimmy Cagney pit-bull, he took the Marine by his remaining arm and with him in tow lunged at the driver. His words and his intent could not be misconstrued, "We're both getting on now, you APA Son of a Bitch, and if you try to stop me, I'll kill you."

For the first time I realized he might do just that, and I became afraid. No shrinking violet, my mother hollered in her deepest voice, "Jim."

It was the Marine who brought the scene to a most uncomfortable end. Not about to be towed anywhere by some insane white guy, he yanked himself from my Father's grasp, gathered himself into an immobile Parade Rest, and simply stated, "Let it go, mister. I don't need no more trouble than I already got."

My father did just that. My mother and brother boarded, and we left the warrior standing erect while citizen stragglers, all white, passed him by and clambered into their comfortable transport. "May God damn them," my Father muttered. We returned to our car and went on home.

NEVER, NE-NE-NE-NE-NEVER HAVE I been capable of anything some objective observer might identify as Normal. Not a normal child. Not a normal preteen. Not a normal teenager. Not even a normal English teacher, a category overstocked with enough very literate oddities to, for themselves at least, establish a most workable anti-normal definition of normalcy. Their brave new world, however, is as formulaic and constrained as is that of the much-maligned, readily identifiable Middle Class. Just a bit weirder. Just a bit more pretentious. And a whole lot more supercilious. So many Ivans to whose society I am incapable of belonging.

But I tried. God knows, how I tried, and as the line goes, "I never failed to fail."[3] There exist dark places and wasted years, some not so dark as others, some not at all wasted. But, I have done much I would be ashamed of, were I capable of shame, and much I should be proud of, were I capable of such emotion. I do not fear the retelling; I do, however, find much of it irrelevant to the unfolding of that part of me which is the subject of this exercise. Thus little reference to the James J. Slattery who wandered about the two decades of the storied sixties and seventies as well as most of the eighties will follow. During the span of almost thirty years I experienced much, including marriage to a wonderful woman whom I betrayed and the fathering of my beloved girls Erin and Shannon. I also lost my father and nearly myself.

By this point in the narrative it must have become apparent that the most influential people in my life were at a far remove from anything anyone would consider ordinary. I do believe, however, that they thought they were in no significant way outside the mainstream. The supra-normalcy they imposed upon me came purely by accident. I will so maintain without even an iota (one of my Father's favorite words) of doubt. Spiritual visitations, criminal associations, passionate love songs, slaughterhouse education, and apocalyptical confrontations.... All a part of everyday living, are they not?

BACK TO THE flow. My life up to Ivan had been neither most simple nor most ordinary. And, at least for those reasons, it had not been even remotely capable of inspiring terror either within myself or some faceless, horrified observer. However, I came to realize that day, that in the sense of spoiled fish wrapped up in pungent marinara it had finally revealed itself to my spiritual palate and forever insinuated its bouquet way up into my sinuses. Thus emerged the very first true epiphany of my as yet youthful life.

For a time that dreary afternoon I reveled in the simple retelling of a life already lived. I could identify. A cousin from Georgia was a federal judge, and a friend would directly follow Ivan's career path from attorney to prosecutor to County Judge. Vaguely I envied them. I knew without doubt that my cousin was my Father's shining example and that the future County Judge was the ideal of my best friend, at the time a Troy police officer. These men were of the law, but somehow they were also above the law. Such seemed to me ideal, and to say I harbored no formless yet very real hopes of somehow breaking free of the shackles of a $7,100.00 *per annum* salary and following in the footprints left by their Italian shoes would be an unforgivable equivocation. After Ivan, however, at least regarding a legal career, Poe's Raven quoth it best, *Nevermore.* Way before the end of Ivan's story, Tolstoy had forced me into my own black sack. His protagonist learns a cruel fact of mankind's existence: any pretense at normalcy is a malicious lie and, in the eternal light of death, not only should there be no Fear, but Fear itself is just another of the deceptions a normal human somehow finds so paradoxically comforting. Such was also my revelation, but I could see no escape from that which I had already become and would continue to become. Somewhere in Section *XI,* I came to realize that I too was Ivan Ilych. But so also were all those others around, above, and below me, lawyers, police, professors, bankers, mechanics, and so many more so completely summed up by their titles, lifestyles, pleasures and pains. I could not in any sort of conscience, good or evil, join them. They had chosen or were in the process of choosing their own existential demise. I would refuse to do the same, but knew my refusal would be in vain. For a brief period of several paragraphs and a fresh hit of Old Granddad, I felt myself, pathetically, more victim than sinner.

Tolstoy, a most spiritual man, makes it almost too easy to sit in judgment not only upon Ivan but his friends and colleagues, his family, the doctor, even his way too shallow religion. In fact the very hope these last two offer is not only pathetic but perhaps unconsciously evil. By the time in my life when I read this I had become, at least to my complete satisfaction, the perfect atheist. I believed in nothing, held nothing sacred, in fact might have considered myself a Nihilist had I not as yet held an abiding love for my baby daughter, my dog, and the rest of my immediate family. Even upon them, however, I placed no value other than as they related to me. To claim my universe was solipsistic might seem too simplistic, yet neither then, nor as I presently reflect, was or am I able to imagine either a person or thing upon whom or which I might have placed even a modicum (another of my Father's favorites) of independent value. Say it. Hear it: My father. My mother. My brothers and sister. My daughter. My friends. My family. My job. My students.... Sometimes only a cliché says it perfectly. I was oh so full of myself.

As the story drew to its close, I found myself enthralled by Ivan's discussion with the Opium inspired *alter-ego* he thought might be his conscience or even God. Through the beneficence of drugs I too had more than once intuited a prismed light at the end of my own world's birth canal, and as day wore down toward evening, I began to envy Ilych's painfully transcendent death throes. In brief, I felt no pity, not even sympathy, in no wise identified with the pathetic and struggling creature Ivan had become. Rather, from somewhere arose the same attractive revulsion for Ivan I felt for another literary character, Gregor Samsa, and something vague yet growing in intensity surfaced like a holy Rambo from out the muck of a polluted and weed choked pond, an insidious assassin sent from somewhere too elsewhere to be imagined, and my smoke died away as ice melted the Bourbon into a watery irrelevance. Tolstoy, damn you and bless you, your story took my life from me. As I read on to the end, your blade slipped between my ribs and into my heart. I died.

Too cynical to be seduced by the "What joy" I was exactly cynical enough to realize the oxymoronic nature of the final sequence: "'Death is finished,' he said to himself. 'It is no more.' He drew in a breath, stopped in the midst of a sigh, stretched out, and died."[4] The other teachers in the department taught this as the salvation of Ivan's soul, the triumphant entry of his spirit into the warm embrace of God, the saints, and Jesus, himself. And, it must be granted, no thinking person, cynical or credulous can rationally deny that the ending of *The Death of Ivan Ilych* contains a revelation of some sort, or that the epiphanic sequence is a spiritual/psychological birthing process replete with impossible to deny references to Christ on the cross. Nonetheless, Ivan still died, and the story offers no indication that he went anywhere but into a blindingly final moment of awareness. In fact, in his other writings Tolstoy never asserts anything other than skepticism, scorn, or even hostility toward the common Christian belief in the afterlife, which delusion allows people to ignore the present actuality of the place of which Jesus spoke and rather to focus upon myriad schemes promising salvation through dogmatic purity and prescribed practices. According to the author, Jesus never taught these things.

In an earlier section I have made mention of an aunt who lavished both her affection and her other earthly resources upon my father. Her name was Maude Nichols, and for the time she was something of a revolutionary figure. As a young woman, somewhere in the vicinity of 1910, she was the first of her gender in the entire county to drive. At the age of twenty-two she traveled the Continent unchaperoned and studied art for two years in Paris. Later on, finding herself isolated among others not of her kind, she found her life's companion in my Great Aunt Margaret, and thus were my parents, an uncle, and an aunt drawn into circumstances far removed from the poor brick-mason's existence of Troy, NY. These most fortunate ones were educated and set upon their myriad paths of worldly success. Only my father failed ever to find that, although, he would claim loudly, often drunkenly, but always proudly that his life far outshone anything mere money could provide. I will not quibble. But I do wonder. He never read Tolstoy, never would have admitted to being anything other than an Irishman, a Catholic, and the husband and father his heart led him to become. Oh yes. One other title these others may have forced upon him. James Joseph Slattery was a consummate binge-drinking alcoholic.

I, as well as my father, have been molded by Aunt Maude, *Alla* as I called her, the result of her singing "La, la, la" to me as a baby. In many respects Alla lives within me, but most relevant to this moment is the nature of her dying. I swear to the God I now believe in that neither of my parents had read *The Death of Ivan Ilych*, most probably were unaware of its very existence, yet somehow they may have known something Tolstoy would have recognized as a transcendent truth, larger than himself or any other person great or small, his work, his nation, perhaps of this world itself. Tolstoy writes of Ivan: "From that moment the screaming began that continued for three days, and was so terrible that one could not hear it through two closed doors without horror."[5] My aunt, the woman who supported my father throughout most of his life, who lived with us from my birth in 1941 until her death in 1963 died in a way most horrifying and especially in one particular aspect most reminiscent of Ivan's experience of the blight we all are born for. For over ten years, beginning with a small "bunch" as my mother termed it, Cancer ate away at Alla's leg until it eventually may have consumed her soul. The first three operations attempted simple removal of the tumors which grew so prominently first upon her ankle and then began to march up her calf. Eventually the doctors amputated her left leg just below the knee. The cancer returned above the amputation site. Again they amputated, and then again, eventually taking hip and all remnants of her limb. Unafraid, she fought; alive as ever, she wheeled herself around in her chair, still the most vital and vibrant of living souls. But, as God willed, at least so my mother declared, the cancer attacked her pelvic organs, and for most of a year Alla was confined to her hospital bed in the upstairs room once hers, then mine, and then hers again.

I was newly married. Had just started school. My wife was a clerk in a Rexall drugstore. My brother John lived with us and we both were beginning college in Mansfield, Pennsylvania. Citing pressing concerns, my mother and father removed themselves to Berlin, NY where my father taught in the local public school. The dying woman was left in the care of a two-hour a day visiting nurse, Margaret her eighty something friend, and my wife, Maureen, who had been taught by the nurse to administer the Morphine injections necessary during those hours when the nurse would not be there. I remember her practicing on an orange. Something positive must have taken hold of her, for several years later she became an RN and developed a rewarding and distinguished career.

They knew what they were doing, my mother and father. Within six or seven weeks It began: A screaming came across our twilit sky one evening while we sat around a table of canned pasta and Sloppy Joes. I had a dog, a large dog, and, at first, I thought he must have gone upstairs and somehow caught his testicles in a door. One long drawn howl followed by a series of shorter yelps froze our greasy forks, locked our greedy elbows. "What the hell's" echoed around our scarred and scabbed board. Again the howl and yips. Forks clattered upon plastic plates. "We'd better go see what's up," someone said. But we already knew. It was Alla, and Hell had opened its gates for her right there in 48 Waln St., Wellsboro, Pennsylvania.

"We'd better call Dr. Prevost," my wife Maureen asserted. We did just that. About half a screaming hour later he arrived, took a listen, injected her with a good quantity of opiate, and increased her prescribed dosage for the future. He spoke not of her prognosis. But we all, except for Aunt Margaret, knew. Her end was upon her. And upon us as well.

In less than a week the screaming came again howling its predatory anthem across our skies. Alla, a shriveled half-woman, insubstantial as a winter's dream, possessing no more vitality than a withered leaf strung from a broken branch, could not possibly have been its source. I could not resist imaginings of the paranormal. We all had seen The Exorcist, and in no time "possession" became a word whispered among us half in jest and half in something approaching conviction. Our comfortable house on 48 Waln Street, once achingly normal, had become the abode of an unquenchable horror, echoing with the cries of a tormented soul wailing its agony as if from deepest Hell itself.

We became convinced that within the husk which once had been our aunt raged a fire of greater than nuclear intensity. That her heart, her mind, her spirit, twisted and blazed but would not be consumed.

The doctor visited every other day or so, but could offer no relief. And would not provide release. Her dosage could not be increased; neither could the intervals between her injections be shortened. Dr. Prevost never said these words, but all his circumlocution meant exactly: "She will have to wait, will have to suffer. Her only hope is death."

It was early spring. The grade school lay at one dead end of our street, the junior high at the other. On any given day a significant number of youngsters would walk past 48 Waln on our side of the street. Not only closed doors but locked shut and drapery drawn windows could not muffle the sound, disguise the terror, or conceal the inhuman suffering within that blighted address. *En masse* the peripatetic scholars detoured themselves around to the other side of the block both morning and afternoon as my aunt's screams, like sentient, malevolent vines awaiting the unlucky passerby whose terror might provide them sustenance, continued to curl about the leafing branches of the great Elms in front of our house.

My brother called my mother. She spoke to my wife. Her only suggestion was an accidental overdose. To her credit or not, I truly do not know, Maureen refused. The suffering continued; the screaming stayed strong.

An adept member of a family of adepts at feeling no pain, until the afternoon with Ivan Ilych, I remembered the evil of those days with a set of emotions ranging from annoyance, through amusement all the way to laughter. A good portion of our family history is constructed of visions of comic horror. The Death of Maude A. Nichols is one of those stories. Among them: My wife, my sister and I standing at the top of the stairway howling in our best Maudlin voices, "Margaret...Margaret...Margaret" over and over until the pathetic old lady had managed to climb the stairs and feel her way along the hallway to her loved one's room. Then the fun truly began. The one-legged, dying woman had run free from patience or even a smidgen of tolerance, but, old and sick as she might have been, never once did she reprimand any of us for our cruelty. Instead she heaped further abuse upon Aunt Margaret, demeaning her with gentle lady obscenities and ridiculing her gullibility. This happened at least once a week over the course of the final month of her dying. Margaret never failed to respond, never recognized her victimization, and always forgave the passionate one left in her most devoted care. We should have been ashamed. Nevertheless, despite now claiming to be exactly that, we continue telling the story at family gatherings, and remain incapable of stifling our laughter as in-laws and prospective members of the tribe silence their own gasps of revulsion and lower their timid eyes.

ONE MIGHT EXPECT that any tale of enlightenment triggered in part by Leo Tolstoy's classic story of Joy and Redemption might include some remorse for past cruelties, especially those imposed upon an innocent and equally devoted female Gerasim. Such, however, was not to be. My realization, enlightenment, if you will, is no less profound for its containing not a grain of compassion, sympathy or pathetic identification with all of doomed humanity. That Saturday I was not transported into the light by such emotions, neither was I brought to tragic awareness by pity and fear. Instead I blindingly recognized my own voice in Christ's cry, *"Eli, Eli lama sabachthani?"* "My God, my God, why have you forsaken me?" (Matthew 27:46)

Growing up Catholic, having been taught Catechism by Sisters of Saint Joseph, I had been classically, or is it operantly, conditioned to bow my head, chin to chest, whenever the name of Jesus was mentioned. Why? Because He came down from Heaven, was born of the Virgin Mary, suffered and died for me. Because of Him, Baptism, one of the seven sacraments, those outward signs instituted by Christ (Nod) to give Grace had already saved us all (Catholics at least) from Original Sin, and through another of His sacraments, "Penance" then, "Reconciliation" now, my personal offenses both mortal and venial would be forgiven, and I would be made worthy, after a brief stop in Purgatory, to enter the Kingdom of Heaven. Jesus died on the cross for me. He suffered and died so that my sins and the sins of all the world might be forgiven. The Perfect Sacrifice, he suffered human pain and gave his human life so that God, our as well as His Father, could in his infinite Mercy find the strict requirements of Divine Retributive Justice satisfied, and finally after our untold centuries of wandering in error and depravity, allow us to escape the torments and fires of everlasting Hell.

As something of a well-read and skeptical teenager, I had begun to question this dogma. Not to mother or father, nuns or priests. I have been at times fooled, but not to my knowledge, limited as it may be, have I become, at least publicly, an actual Fool. Once I did bring my questions up to Mike who merely shrugged, mumbling into his Duquesne something to the effect that he neither knew nor cared with an obscenity of a particularly sexual nature thrown in for emphasis. I was left alone until college. There I found kindred souls. There I learned that skepticism was good and that, religion, especially Catholicism, was an evil delusion. Quickly I flowed through Agnosticism into the great well of Atheism. By my second year I felt I had come into my own promised land and the walls of my enemies had already come tumbling down.

So that Ivan Ilych afternoon I sat alone on the edge of my bed, bag of weed spilling brown Columbian out upon my pillow, Grand Dad adding a sharp touch, a barely muted alcoholic scream, to the intoxicating air. As I watched some seeds like dark tears tumble down into the folds of my wrinkled sheets, I belatedly lunged to contain the potentially disastrous spill. "God damn it," I hollered in an unquiet Irish whisper. As I reached for the treacherous baggie, my hand caught on something adrift in the air, and, instead of securing the spill, blundered knuckles first into the nearly ounce-full container and punched its contents free not only all over my bed but on to the floor as well. The black doghair floor where my Shepherd lay asleep. "Daaaaaaammmmmm," I howled. Just like Aunt Maude as her own life spilled carelessly from her. "Goood daaaammmm it to fucking Helllll," I screeched, and all the afternoon of living in Ivan's opium dream unfolded its ineffable meaning about me. I fell through into absolute certainty.

The Death of Ivan Ilych, Alla's cries of torment, Christ's

passion on his cross.... And my scattered stuff of dreams. They all tell the same idiotic beads. Pain and loss are the truths of our lives. If the Only Begotten Son of God, Jesus Christ, came to earth, suffered crucifixion, and died abandoned so that even we might see, forget the resurrection, the non-existent "promise" of eternal life; even he could not escape pain and death. Rather than bringing hope to our sad existence, He taught us to despair. And if he were not God's son? Well then, who can learn any lesson from him, or Alla, or Ivan other than the same one? We have lost from the first moment we began the game of life. There is nothing to hope for. We will all die. Some will go easier than others, but we will all suffer. So what to do?

I had read Camus' *The Stranger*. Had found it strangely attractive, and in the months after Ivan I understood Meursault's condition for the first time. He would not surrender, would not believe. His sentence of death, to be executed almost at someone else's whim, rather than filling him with Christian despair, liberated him. He, for the first time was free. At that moment, without any conscious reference to Camus, I came to this same awareness. Ironically, at the start, Tolstoy's great spiritual tale drove me further away from anything resembling Christianity. The screams of all the dead and dying echoed long within the empty soul I did not believe I had. All I possessed was the freedom of one who was about to die.

Tolstoy certainly predated Carlos Castaneda, most probably Don Juan as well, but I wonder about the Yaquis and their wisdom as I also wonder about Tolstoy and his Ivan. The Yaqui's knew five coexistent worlds. Most Christians only two. Most Atheists and scientists only one. I am led to wonder, does all the early—prehistoric—knowledge and wisdom of all the world's peoples originate somewhere and sometime which are the same where and whens? Not five. Not two. Not one. Simply all. Are there any *separate* pasts and places at all? I to this date do not know, but as this piece is as much the expression of a developing awareness—knowledge and understanding—of that which may be termed Spirit or God as well as other names too numerous to mention, possibly by the final period of the exercise I shall have achieved that which I seek and will have revealed it to you as well. Anyway, here and now, I am led to assert that in the Yaqui sense of the phrase, Leo Tolstoy both was and is A Man of Knowledge. As such, my misunderstanding of his revelation in no fashion obstructed its power in my life. The words in the paragraphs just prior to this one were the words of that time and of the person bearing both my name and primitive consciousness. As such they speak an essential truth not of who I *am* but of he-who-was-to-become while at the same time always being the one who am *I*. Sounds more than a bit pretentious. But, it says what I mean it to say. Getting it all wrong became the first positive step along the path to eventual understanding.

CHAPTER THREE

The long dark road

THE AGING MAN sits at the bar. His knees press against its splintering face; his elbows weigh hard upon the yellowing top. The sad man awaits his beer. Twelve ounces to move him somewhere else. The thirsty man drinks. Then another. Then another. No more than fifteen minutes have passed. The empty man orders another brew. Nothing seems to work. This next will no doubt fail too. Its toothless mouth clicks against his central incisors; gas pushes from him into the ragged stool. He drinks more slowly. The beer is cold, and so.... No by God, it has happened. His neck flexes, his head thrown back. He takes it all, and the gift is his. No more. Nothing matters. He has entered into a flowered world of alcohol, pizza, perfume, and through the open door, fresh May air. The homeless man has found his home, his garden of earthly delight. Life is good. He smiles and waits at least five minutes before ordering again.

He looks upon his new-dawned, beautifully populated Eden. He is surrounded by the thrumming energies of people. Once again through the simple magic of his own transcendental intoxication, he is inspired by the music from hidden speakers all of which turn his passive sitting away from the pointless contemplation of his lost state back to the first dawn of all possibility. The people move, barkeeps in multiple ways, bar drinkers still save for elbows and mouths, and people come and go, the living flow of light and life, shadow and substance playing about the floor, the walls, the entire blessed field of his senses. He feels himself begin to rise. Feels the weightless moment of flight upon him. He is ready. The holy road lies straight and clear before his unscaled eyes.

The one beside him stands and leaves with two companions. The innocent Adam is granted a wider vista. Down the bar and around to its end stands a tall, dewbright rose. He maybe remembers her. She looks his way and then away. No sign of recognition. He still must remember her; he just doesn't. Another beer will help. And an old fashioned glass of blackberry brandy to steady him. She will notice. Will see the man he is.

Slowly this time he sips the brandy, gazing across the glass at his rose. She is whispering to two friends the way women sometimes do. She is deliberately ignoring him. He takes a bold swallow of his Budweiser and begins an animated conversation with Bruce the bartender. He knows them all. He is a regular. Respected. She will see. Another joins in.

Boston will do it this year.

Bullshit.

An hour and a half have passed over the space of seven words. The bewitched one looks his flower's way. She has faded into another time.

THERE WAS A time when she or some multifoliate sister of hers had not faded with the sunset, when rather the promise of eternal May, of golden light lavished not just upon but somehow radiant from within her had offered its dark welcome, the root of too much Joy for any Ivan ever to have experienced. They had shared not beer but alternating bites of miniature Peanut Butter cups and peppermint patties after some class or other. Perhaps Contemporary Novel. And the mingled sweetness of their mouths as they kissed in the front seat of someone's car, shared a toke or two of Colombian, and, despite his general distaste for the stuff, a little hit of Cousin Cocaine.

Is it possible that now she doesn't remember? That, he can't imagine how, he has somehow offended her? He cannot remember. It had happened once. Had she expected more? If so, why had she become so mute in class, left so hurriedly after dismissal? Surely he had done nothing wrong.

It had been her at the end of the bar. He was certain. Wasn't he?

ANOTHER DAY, ANOTHER Holy Grail waiting to be found. His mind made clear by some very potent Black Beauties and 151. Another blonde. Green eyes this evening time. December has come. Christmas lights have encircled trees, framed windows, and begun the carols of a season even more merry than its predecessors. This girl is more than fine. She could be a model. She is his.

He spies her upon first entry. Through the door she slides. He is prompted to ignore her. Something secretive has hold of her attitude, dampens down her motion. She is becoming shadow, flickers once upon the wall then is no more. Damn. Who would have guessed? Hallucinations from Amphetamines and Rum? He ought to write it down. He could be a poet or even a novelist if he wanted to. He has to pee. He can ask Bruce for a pen and napkin afterward. Damn it, he will write it down. A couple of words, a bit of insight. Who knows?

He is just emerging from the men's room filled with the effluvia of creation when he hears those first notes, the first words.

Damn.... The drug and booze have produced nothing. She is here after all. Has played his—their—song. Highway 101, *Whiskey, if you were a Woman*. What that says about him and her is immaterial. She is here. She is happy. Her green eyes just might blaze sunlight yellow in the parking lot darkness. And this one will scream.

ANOTHER NIGHT. HE was drunk last night for the exhibition he had hosted. His wife and best friend had cared for him. Had more than adequately handled things. Who gives a damn? Art for the masses is like dogshit on a sidewalk. We all see. We all understand. And it stinks. This Jazz night he is drunk as well, but no longer belligerent. A friend of a martyr's name slumps in a corner dribbling from his open mouth, his eyes stark against his Celtic skin and themselves drooling. A bottle leans uneasily upon his open palm. The musicians are gone, but the music lives on. Rock and Roll. The man dances with the woman. Their pelvises move in unison. Her meager breasts brush soft against his shirtless chest. He pauses to drink. She sinks down. And they are gone. The friend in the corner cares not a bit despite the fact that she is his.

ANOTHER DAY, ANOTHER room, this one called the "reproduction room" by the faculty. It is a place with a machine for making copies. He leans against the hulk of Xerox. The four women crowd together in the doorway. He has come here with them. Wishes he could leave with but one.

Her given name is the same as that of the Jazznight succubus. Otherwise they are not at all alike. Jazz was thin and something of a wisp. This one is curved, round and small with professionally done hair, short and light-brown, skin tone something like the Boston Cream within a sweet dessert. And her dress.... Oh, his great and nonexistent god, all women should accouter themselves so. Her dress might have hung plain upon anyone else. Upon her it assumes an air of no-nonsense professionalism. The little neck loops just below the tiny horns of her collarbone. Her breasts, well concealed and obviously well-restrained, shout out their maternal possibilities. Her hips the same. Wide and welcoming they announce the give and take of the most basic female sexuality. But most delectable of all are her legs. From out one corner of her hem peeks the tiniest wisp of pure white lace. And on her calves tapering to slim ankles glimmers pale nylon, so much more than nude that "nude" can only speak of concealment. The man can only imagine. She must be wearing garters and old-fashioned stockings. Such is the only possibility. And her shoes? Heels like daggers. He can feel those limbs wrapped about him, the harsh footwear cruel against his skin.

She is married. He knows her husband well. But, he must have this goddess....

ANOTHER HOLY ONE awaits. He begins to plot his strategy.

"I will give you happiness," a voice asserts.

The man scans about him. The women are unmoved. The holy lady smiles some secret into their made-up faces. Maybe a flashback of some sort. She will make him happy, not the voice so decidedly male. Resuming the immediate future he imagines her, small beneath him, those legs....

"All you must do is say 'yes' and I will give you everything you are now missing, things even you cannot imagine."

"What?" the man must ask aloud.

The women grow quiet. And, he will always swear, so does the world. Awaiting his answer?

"All you need do is say 'yes' and agree to let me provide. Will you do that?"

Visions of riotous women, real life become an LSD fantasy, intoxicants beyond even his imaginings jumble about like elements of a Pollock within his consciousness. Of course he will. "Yes," he says.

FROM THEN ON, nothing goes well. At least so he thinks. He never has more than a passing smile with the latest addition to his pin-up fantasies. At least, that is, in the flesh. He begins drinking in the morning. Is more often intoxicated on the job. Even his favorite bar-owner asks his wife if something might not be wrong with him. His everyday becomes horror when it has managed to escape from terror. He envisions the dying Ivan Ilych whenever in something of a less than insane state he is able to interact in any sort of even minimal way with his wife and children. He is sorry for them. But he continues hurting everyone.

Jazz Girl has become a pest. She gives him what he wants less and less more and more; he wonders how he can rid himself of her.

The afternoon of 4 May, 1989 he finds himself, after the previous evening's drunken poetry reading, again intoxicated, in the middle of Troy's Broadway arguing at full voice with a deaf versifier who refuses to believe that he cannot write poetry by virtue of the fact that he has no sense of sound. The signer has given up. The deaf man is angry and drunk. This is going to come to blows. A cop slows his car. The combatants reconsider. The man returns home.

A FEW WEEKS earlier, surprisingly sober for a Friday morning. Almost at the top of his imaginary game, the man strolls into an upstairs cafeteria for a meeting with a colleague and some strange, no doubt deranged, survivor of two wars and twenty two years in the Marine Corps, who thinks he might have a talent of sorts for the theatre and who, best friend of a good friend, is looking to the man for employment. He sits at a table, at least fifty years old, red hair growing dark with age, a few traces of old-dog gray at its edges. He is talking aggressively across the table at Will, looks the man's way, halts in mid gesture and stares. No expression. Just stares.

The man knows Marines, active as well as retired, and does not flinch. He too can stare. And does.

Something like the first appearance of sun amid deconstructing storm clouds, a tracing of beneficence softens not just his features but, as would have the sun, supplants the harsh light of the room, and to the man at least, at least for a time, the dim bulb of reality itself. No wonder Will and Jack have spoken so highly of this Red. This morning might just hold some promise.

The man reaches the table, prepares to sit.

Before that can happen, Red John blurts in no unfriendly sort of way. "What the hell happened to your face?"

The man does not speak of this. To anyone. Not wife. Not children. Not you. And absolutely not to some stranger sitting in a community college cafeteria, drinking tea, not coffee, now looking tired before him.

"Why?" the man asks. "I got somethin' on it?"

"Sorry," smirks Red. "Just wondering. None of my business really. Just wondering...."

Will breaks in. Lightens the mood, and not much transpires. The man gets coffee. He does need an assistant. Will excuses himself. John is appalled by the salary.

"Fifteen-thousand dollars? That's an insult. Will said it wouldn't be much. But fifteen grand...."John's continuing unemployment assured, the two chat for a few minutes.

"Gotta go," the Marine states while looking at his watch. "Got a meeting at eleven. AA. Ever been to one?"

The man would rather go to a Pentecostal, kill-me-Lord or maybe even a Jehovah's meeting. But he is determined to be polite. "Little too much Marine Corps?" he asks.

"Tell you something," John answers. "I've maybe been to every country in this world and don't remember any of them."

They both laugh.

On his way, John arises, offering a hand. Not to shake. He hands the man a card. "Here's my name and two numbers," he states, no accusation in his voice or on his face. "Ever need something," give me a call.

He is gone.

THE EMPTY MAN sits at a table, out of place but convenient, in his front room. *Born to be Wild* cranks unheard behind the drapes closing him from the day. The phone rings. He stumbles off to answer. It is a friend, suicidal and in some sort of drugged haze threatening self destruction. "Go ahead" the man mumbles and hangs up.

"Who was that?" calls his wife.

He need not answer. Never does. Does not.

Instead he takes the clunkykreme handset back to his table, mumbles through his wallet.

Calls the number he finds there.

FROM THAT EVENING forward both alone and in the company of much professional and not so professional advice, the man exists in a world without alcohol or drugs of any abusable kind. He is clean and sober. Especially in the beginning he resents this but soon embraces the change, soon realizes an awakening. Someone in one of the multitudinous rooms through which he has passed has stated without inflection of doubt that the first day of real sobriety, whatever that means, for him was a rebirth and at his moment of reemergence he found himself still a teenager. Maybe sixteen. The man had to laugh. What idiocy.

The voice of the reproduction room does not comment. Eventually the man will find its message huge upon his landscape as are those digital flickerings now so prominent up and down the streets and towers of Midtown Manhattan. However, he is as yet unaware that his life is about to become a Times Square of not-so innocent delight packaged in a Disney wrapper of insidious seduction. Sobriety is God Damned Dreary. Or so he thinks. And then....

Ninety days and more than ninety meetings later, AA Boot camp graduation upon him, he awakens to a most troubling fact. The man has become almost seventeen. Or is he even younger?

His chip tells him three months. The meeting ends. He has shared at length. John has nodded his approval. The man, always glib, always easy spoken and usually too verbose, has wowed the McCarty Avenue Meeting. He cannot remember a word, sentence or theme of what it is he said. But they loved it. What a fraud. He grins to himself, embracing the profoundly vacuous comments of the other alcoholics, endures their flabby shakes and fleshy, boney, too-intimate hugs. All but John's.

"Think you've fooled us, don't you? Not me you haven't." He laughs so hard his Santa-belly shakes like the poem has said. "You might make it. But you sure as hell ain't even close yet.... Now, let's go get a meeting after this one where you can listen rather than blab. You might learn something."

The man just has to love John. The truth sucks. But those who say it stand at the top of all else.

A YEAR LATER the man still knows more than he will say, says less than he would were it not for a fear of alienating John. The evening prior to his present he has stood in a circle. The sheep are praying the "Our Father." The woman to his left is frail, with the emaciated look of one much beyond anorexia, perhaps into the later stages of cancer—ovarian he would have guessed had he bothered to. "Your Kingdom come," she squeezes his hand, a tiny pressure of almost no note at all. Something sings into his palm and up his arm. He holds on tight as if they both are in danger of washing away. "For thine is the kingdom," her hand wilts in his. He tightens his grip. "And the power," something moves from deep within him. He is hard, but not with lust. "And the glory," They are abandoned. Lost. "Forever," She pulls loose at "Amen."

"You hurt me," she breathes in a voice too soft to hear but which may as well have blasted itself past his bursting drums and into a consciousness deeper than any sense may address.

"Sorry," he mumbles, and stumbles away into the night.

CHAPTER FOUR

an empty vessel

THUS BEGAN MY search for something—I would not say God—more. Something that moment in that basement room had struck into flame. The friend, who had not committed suicide, who, unbelievably had found wisdom in my so casual "Go ahead," and who for some time had been prospecting in one form or another for Taoist enlightenment, had offered hints along the way of our recent past. I recognized a title, *The Tao Te Ching*. I bought the book.

"DO YOU BELIEVE in the afterlife?" I oh so pointedly asked my father as we sat in summer sunshine. Eighty degrees in the diminishing little town of Berlin, New York, he nonetheless huddled within the expanding fabric of one of his signature white sweatshirts. Everything for him by this time had become too large. And it had been little more than a week in the process.

We all knew he had a serious, almost debilitating hernia. My first memory of his condition stretches all the way around the little pool of our experience to a further shore, tropical, downright hot. The crab I had fished from the Gulf clattered sluggishly at the galvanized pail in which I kept him. My first pigeon innocently waded through the webs of thread I had carefully woven about the crumbs scattered upon the alleyway as bait. I caught him too. He was one angry and violent bird, pecking at my careful fingers as I sought to unwrap his entangled feet, his close-bound wings. They said I couldn't do it—catch him that is. I did though; I just couldn't free him. Eventually I crushed him with the new

Adirondack Bat my Uncle, the plant manager, had brought me. The next day my crab was dead as well.

At the time my mother's recriminations seeming to my five-year-old intelligence without logic or merit, I quietly asked her, "But aren't they better off in Heaven?"

Alla heard and laughed softly and somehow politely. My father smiled his *that's my boy* smile, and my mother withdrew—in defeat I was certain. The next day my Father went off to someplace called The Hospital for a hernia operation. What that was I did not know. He was gone for a long time and returned weak and unable to remain awake for more than a couple of hours. Three months later, on our trip back north, something strained; something ruptured; the repair failed. For the next twenty-plus years he would wear a belt of some insane structure and become adept at pushing his intestines up out of his scrotum and back into his pelvic cavity. Who needs doctors anyway? Just a bunch of quacks.

Twenty-four years into another time, another July, another place, the same people. The five-year-old father of two awaits an answer.

"No," was all my father said. He coughed. His eyes turned inward. Away from me. Somehow children know that pigeons and crabs must die, even that people are mortal, at least most of them. But not my father. Ten days prior to our conversation the doctor he had consulted concerning possible surgery had told him his heart was far too far gone for such elective vanity. The recommendation was made that he immediately see a Cardiologist. An appointment had been scheduled, had been canceled. My father would go to an appliance manufacturer in Coudersport, Pennsylvania where they would outfit him with the appropriate support. What do those fool doctors know anyway?

I must have asked the question because of some premonition, perhaps a Martha McInroy Slattery moment of enhanced perception. I do not know. Maybe Pa's weakness and impending dissolution had become too blatant to any longer be ignored. I did not know and did not care to know. In one second's time I had grown overfull with some rancid mixture of disgust, betrayal, and profoundly still anger. "Did you ever?" I demanded.

"No," he said again.

"So why," the not yet fully realized alcoholic raged beneath anyone's possible perception, "did you make us go to Mass all those Sundays? All those years?"

"We are Catholics," he replied softly but this time directly into my eyes.

"What good is that, any of it, if there's no afterlife...no heaven? The Catholic Church is a lie."

Once, when both of us were far too intoxicated even to be standing, he fully grown, I about to become a senior in high school, he had kept reaching around my mother's shield and punching me in the side of the head. I grew tired. And so I responded. A good left hook and he was down for longer than I remember. I went on to bed. The next morning he woke me, gave me fifty dollars and banished me from his household. Fifty dollars was a lot of money in 1958. It took a friend and me on the road to Atlantic City where we indulged in beer and low-quality weed, saw the Diving Horse and listened to Xavier Cugat, made enemies of some friendly prostitutes, and, still drunk three days later, hitched ourselves home. They never kicked any of us out of the house again. I had taught them that lesson well. Neither did my father hit me again, I think for fear that he would have to kill me.

That 1971 afternoon I thought perhaps things had somehow mutated exactly to that most ugly state. He was just too weak to do it, and so he snarled, an old bulldog, distempered as all hell, "Don't you ever abandon our Church. My father never did. Nor his father before. You're a Catholic, goddamn it. Never forget it." He had begun to roar like some old tuskless walrus; my mother came upon us as he was attempting to rise from the white wicker lawn chair in which he had been sitting. "You," he hollered. "Get your APA ass back inside. This is between us." But then he failed to extricate himself from his white woven cell, and falling back, snored deep and angry breaths while his blood-backed hands clutched futily into fists.

For the first and last time in my life I pitied him. I was not as yet prepared to accept my own decreasing days of wine and roses as in any way tied up with the processes he had already passed through, nor was I at all repentant. "Fuck the Catholic Church," I thought quite verbally, but from my mouth slipped, "I'm sorry, Pa. I just don't get it that's all." I rose like a gentle, unhurried breeze from my own wicker nest and clasped his shoulder in an appropriately distant gesture of concern, at which point his sagging face rose up to meet me and somehow I discovered myself, not really me, it just couldn't have been, burying my own cheek next to his, and, turning my face into that once bull-great neck, I kissed the flap of flesh hanging there.

The day went on for several hours more, including a family meal with my uncle and aunt, brothers and sister, in-laws and children around the great long table. Mashed potatoes, steak, and jokes were passed about in profusion, and then I was home. Our final words had been spoken.

Three days later in a motel room upon a mountain top in northern Pennsylvania my mother awoke to find James Joseph Slattery dead beside her.

It is claimed by many that the death of Jesus sealed the deal and we now have become, some would say all of us, the forever blessed Children of God. I would never have ventured there in 1971 and, despite having taken a leisurely tour of those climes several years afterward, have not an iota of regard for such credulousness, even in my present state. I will, however, assert that through my Father's last passion enacted within a narrow valley of no portentous shadow, his most forgettable front yard, and his death somewhere not much closer to God, came an essential identification which I neither wish to nor am able to deny. I watched others fall apart during the immediate aftermath of his dying. I shed not a tear. I have observed the others move on over their own horizons, some into the bleary fogs of dysfunctional adulthood and old age. Many into death's somewhereorother kingdom. I myself have moved on in many pleasurable as well as soul-destroying directions and toward at best an ever-shifting, uncertain finality or lack of same. One aspect of the phantasmagoric jumble, however, remains constant. Nearly one year to the day from our conversation, my Father's words exploded within the cabin of my little pickup; clear and strong as never had they been uttered, they commanded, "You're a Catholic, goddamn it. Never forget it."

It was not just his voice strong and alive. It was all of him. I drifted off to the side of Oakwood Avenue and cried, mourning him—my loss—for the first time. He was wrong. He is not gone. And I am a Catholic, goddamn it. And I will never forget that.

THAT IS TO say: I am a Catholic who rarely attends Mass. I am a Catholic who denies anything to do with the Pope other than his common humanity, and who will no longer even bother to disagree with the *Magisterium*. I have, however, felt my soul ascend toward Heaven wrapped in the cloths of incense and litanies of mystical substance, have prayed alone in cathedrals where the candle glow of divinity, the forgotten whispers of prayers, long ago said, and the echoes of hymns of substance so ancient as to defy modern reduction have taken me for some temporal moment into the great continuum of the dimensions as yet unknown to most of mankind.

Such is the Catholic Church to me. It is intertwined with who I am, with whatever it may be I shall become. However, I do not *follow* its teachings, do not accept or recognize its authority. Simply put, the mysticism associated with the very earliest of my religious experiences, those I misunderstood and prematurely rejected, is a path toward enlightenment I have chosen to follow, and that road, as Robert Hunter has said, is for my steps alone. Thus for me Catholicism is the Tao. Christ, the founder of it all, my Guide. But I race ahead of myself along a downhill path toward nothing.

The Tao is the Catholic Church, yes, but it is so ineffably much more than that. An early devotee of The Doors, I at the time would have championed LSD as the portal to everything beyond the everyday. My first mistake. Drugs alter who we are without any gift of wisdom; their visions, forgive me Don Juan, are chemical illusions, and the doors they open are into a place, perhaps at times attractively schizophrenic, but always illusory. Jim moved himself to a less circular path and I hope he found a door into vision his music and his drugs never seemed to give him.

One might be inclined to view the preceding paragraph as denial of a classic piece of wisdom, "Every way is the way," but such is not the case. My friend the suicidal Taoist has on more than one occasion and in more than a single way claimed: *Every path we follow, every road we travel, even those ending in darkness, or bramble choked impassibility, every step we must retrace, each mountain we must climb again is the true and only way for us. Some may find the easy way, and for them that is the right way. For you,* he would say to me, *the way will never be easy, and even though short will ever be long. Such is the way.* I do not argue. The Catholic Church and Jesus Christ, Secular Humanism and Richard Dawkins. Every way at least might be the way, if not for me, certainly for some other.

Pamela

A SHORT MOMENT past the first moment of my sobriety, I, a maturing eighteen-year-old in the AA sense of the passage of our formative years, first entered the first class of the rest of my life. *Introduction to the Theatre* was a course I had instituted as a direct result of my early fascination with the dramatic arts and an undergraduate course in theatre history. I had been teaching two sections, one an amalgam of disinterested nursing and Phys-Ed students, the other a soon to become disillusioned cadre of hopeful actors, directors, and other dramatic personae. My life had become sunnier, and, for the first time possibly since I had begun my career at the college, I was profoundly disinterested in the array of hopeful female faces smiling up at me. There was a new someone I had great hopes of replacing my old one with. She was a former student then living in Florida. We had plans. This class might just be my last. At least in Troy, New York.

Yet I still had a semester, perhaps a full school year to go. And I required a secretary. My artistic workload had become burdensome even for this one who now worked sober seven days a week, eight to ten hours a day (In my memory at least). And each class required both time and intellectual focus as well as the mindless chores of grading exams and recording innumerable minutia of the most inane nature for the department. I needed a secretary who would work hard, work long, and who would not trouble the other one I was becoming. And so it came to pass that in the first of my late August classes I asked if someone might be interested.

Pam raised her hand. And that, dear reader, has made all the difference.

She was eighteen, I soon to be forty-nine. Her clothes were inexpensive to a fault. And she was from Berlin, the adopted home of my nomadic family as well as the hometown of my first wife. Her father had been my parents' paperboy. She just, absolutely, positively, and categorically would not do.

But she smiled, and, even though I did not recognize the moment at the moment, I no longer belonged only to myself.

Pam.

ACROSS THE NORTH AMERICAN continent and all around the whole fat globe of twelve or twenty-four-hour timepieces, from The Prime Meridian to International Dateline, Westward from now to then and East into tomorrow, somewhere within all these wheres two alcoholics converse, and one, hopelessly in need of comfort and love is admonished by his wiser, more experienced comrade, "Don't let a woman (or a man) become your Higher Power." The God of our understanding should not be simply the possessor of our preferred assortment of sexual characteristics.

I knew this—believed it. And so it took some time for my conversion from recovery orthodoxy. Deliberately I ignored her charms, could not have said with any significant degree of certainty whether her eyes were brown or hazel. For all I knew they were blue. She was a kid. And besides, she had a boyfriend. And I was still juggling paramours. And I was still full-time into AA. And she was eighteen. Eighteen. No day-to-day surfer of the potentially lethal swells of sobriety can possibly handle any of the hassles even the most casual of relationships with such a one would involve. She might as well have been a forgotten apple hanging from the branch of a forbidden tree.

Unobtrusive. She came early, worked hard, and stayed late. She was quiet to the point of effacing herself right out of range of any conscious perceptions of mine. Yet she sat reliably present at her desk throughout September and most of October, the computer alive before her, her smile always asserting the something I was missing. But I had missed much and missed none of it at all. Her hair was black. That much I knew.

One afternoon, the sun fading the year toward Halloween, after a brief professional conference with a colleague, he, just 90 days sober and in need of some more personal assistance than could be anonymously discussed with Pam present, I suggested our going for coffee. We went. I told him some day-at-a-time truthful fiction, shook his hand, and then was presented with one more AA opportunity.

"You having a thing with that girl in your office?" he casually asked.

"Who, Pam?" I chuckled. "Not a chance. She's only eighteen, you know."

The colleague, ten years younger than I seemed not at all phased. "You wouldn't mind then...if I asked her out. She's pretty hot, you know."

As if I had never heard the woman/Higher Power warnings, I simply answered, "No. Go ahead. I got no interest in her."

The fact is, the soon to relapse alcoholic never proposed a date, but his interest prompted me to take a much closer look at the little girl sitting in my office.

Surprise!

Something moved within me. Was it my spirit or hers? Was it Something else? In light of my later awareness of the coexistent states we term reality, the "other" dimensions of an unrecognized here and now, I would venture to answer: "All of the above." I could assert that Pam is my angel sent from Heaven, that her soul is every bit as old as mine, that my spirit hungered for companionship and Pam's responded. I could even say that as much as I needed someone she did as well and that the moment was of her creation. More confidently, I conjecture that God must be chuckling at my confusion. The answer is so simple. Too simple to explain. Let it be said instead that in the ultimate reality of which I, like Wordsworth, glimpse but fleeting intimations, the questions do not exist and the matters with which they deal are of no matter whatsoever. Across a dirty vinyl floor and through the dustmote atmosphere of a blockgray office, a spark, an infinite wave of consciousness, intertwined with another of its kind within the presence of an immortal illumination issuing from everywhere both under and beyond the sun.

If God is love, and he just may be, then his presence filled the room.

Intellectually, I have dispensed with the notion of lineality as much as is possible as it relates to my part in this delusional world of comic illusion. To say I accomplished that feat some years ago would both be accurate and ludicrous. Truthfully, we poor humans are incapable of relating to the universe which may or may not be around us, to each other, or even to ourselves without submitting to the inexorable straight ahead march of time. Some time ago I happened upon an interesting discussion of the unidirectionality of time. It all concerned the concept of *Time's Arrow*. In the course of the discussion, the question arose, "Why must it always aim toward the future?" No law of physics demands this. In fact, there is no reason why time could not move in the opposite direction. "Backwards," we would say.

At this point, I cannot help but recall Einstein's letter to the family of his dead friend, Michele Besso. "Now he [Besso] has departed from this strange world a little ahead of me. That means nothing. People like us, who believe in physics, know that the distinction between past, present, and future is only a stubbornly persistent illusion."[6] It is this very real "illusion" my association with Pam has caused me to reconsider. Much like the Agnostic upon the verge of atheism which I once was, I feel compelled to question the phenomenological reality I once found such a powerful presence that I could no longer accept the immaterial, the spiritual, the divine.

I have read of auras, human energy fields all the way to Don Juan's egg-people emitting fibrous spikes of light and energy that only those who can see see. None of these concepts describes the gentle and eternal force which allows me to call it Pam. She is more than I am able to describe, yet she is also a profoundly simple woman, and now mother, the very essence of everything those nouns denote. For a time, well after our first acquaintance, I was prone to call her my gift from God, a status she vigorously denied.

"You don't know me," she would say. And, in terms of all the incidentals so many of us consider the bulk of reality, she was right. But I assert and affirm that that day in my fading office when first I *saw* her eyes, I knew more about the both of us than any Horatio and his philosophers could ever even surmise. She is not Goddess; neither is she just Mother, Wife, or Angel. She is Pam. And she led me to God. She is Pam. And she has come back from some time before or perhaps over from some one-hundred-eighty-degree rotational gyre of perpendicular intersections of the time we all inhabit and which is nothing of the sort we think it to be. She could have been born of woman in the year 1971 and grown to maturity as do most human beings. I do not know. Her mother is dead, but her father says so. Anyway, no matter from whence she came, Pam led me to God and away from the vague desert of waterless illusion in which I had been wandering. Even after 1988 and the Reproduction Room.

First, she merely took me to...

Nan's House

BERNIE LOVED HER granddaughter possibly as much as if not more than Susan, her daughter and Pam's mother. The girl could at times seem the second coming of Susan, especially this evening, the Grafton breezes shifting clouds and their shadows about the unlighted house, a car, far-off, the sound of its tires lonely, tired, and in some vague sort of way sad. Like that passing song, the girl stood in and out of sight, a fleeting glimpse, perhaps only possible at the periphery, and brought her mother's darkness to the cheerful kitchen, the hearty essence of fresh cornbread no defense against this sad intrusion.

Always it would not be her. Bernie loved the girl. Her life

brought love and hope to the aging widow, the grieving mother. But not enough. Truly, nothing could ever be enough. Susan had passed. To be with Jesus. Whatever the devil that meant.

Bernie could not help it. As a tear escaped her eye, a tear lengthened itself across the inner heart of her blood choked heart, the tiniest chuckle escaped her firm-set lips, and the girl emerged softly into the sudden flare of light the newly unoccluded sun struck through her west-facing windows.

"What, Nan?" the young one asked. "What's so funny?" And the poor little dear could not help but so aching obviously check herself over for the comic flaw in her appearance which had made her Nan laugh so.

"It's you," Bernie smiled. "I was just thinking of an old song, *You are my Sunshine*, and just then the real sun came out just as you came out to the kitchen." With that, she gave her Pam the longest brief hug her nature would allow. "How about some tea...for you and your friend? He likes tea, doesn't he? I got no coffee. Maybe Sanka...."

The man is in the other room, uncomfortable in a comfortable chair set face-to-face with a jumpy TV playing on its lone channel a Billy Graham Crusade. The man is no longer an atheist, but neither is he some Born Again yoyo. Foolish as the Catholic Church can be, this *Christian Shit* is downright insane, foolish, but not even in the least positive application of the term. Gautama Buddha once said something about a fool who knows he is a fool being truly a wise man while a wise man who considers himself wise is truly a fool. The man loves such concepts, but those who fool themselves through the shallowest literal readings of scripture and the most pathetic hopes for an after-life and some insane sort of eternal reward are not the sort of whom the Master spoke. They live in the land of the earthworm and their emergence into the sunlight will be like unto the lot of their hermaphroditic brethren who on a bright spring morning, after a night of warm showers find themselves by the thousands crawling across deserts of black top and concrete, slowly frying into flat and withered, empty sacs of what once was life. Too foolish to even be worthy of the name.

And here he sits, staring at Billy Graham, the patron earthworm of them all, calling them all to the light, his fool's voice become their fool's call unto the fool's altar. They snake their way toward a deadly light of their own choosing. They are the empty seeking sustenance, the night-crawlers in search of day, the lower than fools on their way to an elevation known as death. In his old and bitter way, the man allows a familiar rush of scorn to prompt a silent laugh.

How can every way be the way? Surely these vermin will never get to the place to which they think they are going. They are already corpses. Can't the goddamn fools see that?

"Come down," the bespectacled preacher calls. "Open your hearts to Jesus. Come on down...Jesus loves you. Simply give yourself.... Open your hearts.... And to you out there within the sound of my voice, in your living rooms and kitchens, your somehow empty homes despite the luxury all around you. Hear me. Say this simple prayer with me...." The prayer is something like, "Jesus, come into my life. I give my will and myself to you. Forgive me, Jesus, and save me."

People on the screen are weeping, shouting, laughing and embracing. Sounds like and looks like an AA meeting the man thinks. They say AA's a spiritual program. Maybe.... For some reason he does not scoff any more. "Anyway...."

The damn fool preacher once again addresses his television audience. Requests again that they follow him in the prayer. He knows not why, but the man mumbles the words.

Just as he finishes, Pam slips into the room. "Nan wonders if you'd like some tea and cornbread?"

"Yes, thank you," the man replies. "Three sugars...OK?"

Derek

ABOUT A YEAR after his Billy Graham non-experience and immediately following a trip to Russia succeeded a few months later by a week in Ireland, the man began to experience a familiar emptiness, and a profound need for something to fill the void. He had Pam, her love and her gentle concern as well as her challenging intellectuality. He also had begun attending her Baptist church on occasion. But inside him the Dark Well grew, threatening to turn something the wrong side out. He would not drink again. But there was much else he might do.

As luck, or is it God, would have it, a friend, The English Department Chair at the college, had enrolled in a Japanese Karate school, had found it challenging, had found the *Sensei* exceptionally talented. She encouraged the man, who she knew had trained as a boxer, studied *Tai Chi*, as well as traditional *Kung Fu*, and had dabbled in *Wing Chung*, to try a class with her. He did. She soon dropped out. The man, however, found fulfillment of a sort neither the Chair nor *Sensei* Hoffman, not even the man, himself, ever would have imagined.

The man is not nor ever has been a half-way guy. One week into *Kokorokan Karate*, a hard-core Japanese style, the group was subjected to *Sensei* Hoffman's infamous Thousand Kick Drill. The man did not know all the techniques and so he was reduced to seemingly infinite repetitions of *hiza-geri, mae geri, mawashi-geri,* and *yoko-geri,* knee, front, roundhouse, and sidekicks. His classmates were required to execute a greater variety, in keeping with their knowledge and abilities, but they all somehow forced out the same number. One Thousand.

The scene in the locker-room afterward reflected many truths dependent upon the student flashing into close up. The man knew none of their names but for the first time began to differentiate each from the other, not by appearance, nor by any of the usual physical characteristics which so often mask us as individual. Not by facial features, body type or even the differing vocal qualities. There was something else he at first could not identify yet which he recognized as a familiar feature of his overall perception of human beings ranging from his mother and father, through Mike and Pug, his brothers and sisters, his children, two of whom remained unborn, and right up tight to Pam. At some he smiled a supercilious sneer, those in whom he recognized the first signs of withdrawal, a soft form of cowardice, of weakness in need of rationalization; toward others he tentatively beamed a smile indicative of some degree of brotherhood. Upon himself he looked with satisfaction. Surely he who sired him would have been well pleased. He had done it. And he seemed much less the worse for wear than any of the others, at least blue-belts all. His legs were tired. His spirit was strong. He had triumphed. He was The Man.

At that moment of transcendent egoism an awakening blew in from the *dojo* floor. The man knew not his name, but around his waist he wore a newly-earned black belt. He was *Shodan*, only first degree, but to the man any black-belt signified achievement and status perhaps unattainable by a mere mortal. Part of the reason for this exalted view came from popular mythology, but part also resulted from the man's having observed this particular warrior in action a few evenings previous. The man had arrived early for his class, and the prior class, one for advanced students, had been just finishing *kumite*. This particular black-belt had stood before a hulking, absolute polar bear of a brown-belt and had kicked, punched, swept, and totally confounded him. If anything martial can truly be an art, then this warrior was also an artist. And he looked the part. Honestly, thought the man, no little bit in thrall to awe, the *shodan* should make a movie.

This particular day, the ruin which thumped down upon the bench between two rows of equally battered lockers would be in no one's movie. Its black hair remained only half captured by its rubber band; the piercing eyes had developed folds theretofore unnoticed; the mocha complexion had turned a slippery mottle of cancerous pearl and alcoholic rosacea, and his lithe torso had lost its tone. Even his *obi* drooped. The *shodan* had been more totally defeated than had even the weakest of the junior students. The man could not help but stare at the fallen one with no mere smidgen of dismay. Could he possibly be the fittest one there?

The defeated warrior had not lost all sense. After no short pause, he cleared his eyes and looked dark into the man's own. Immediately the man knew: this guy was not defeated; he was proud; he was victorious. But, he was nothing but the jumbled wreckage of the star he once had been. What could he be missing, the man wondered.

A small drop of sweat dripped from the *shodan's* aquiline nose and the look of the predator returned to his countenance. His form reassembled something inside, and a look of recognition cleared his face.

"I watched you," he said. "Your form is awful, but you got it done. Now listen to me...." He leaned forward and lowered his voice. "Don't ever save yourself again."

The man could not accept what he was hearing. He had done all the kicks; others had not. He had run several marathons and prided himself on his ability to outlast any ordeal. He had done just that. Better than the pretender before him; that was for sure.

The black-belt laughed harshly. "I know...you think you're cool because you did it all and not only survived but walked off the floor with energy to spare." A longer pause. "That," *sempai* Martone emphasized with three stiff fingers to the man's sternum, "is what you did wrong." He continued in a voice loud enough for all to hear, "The only way to do this right, whether you're here for your first class or have a black belt, is to go all-out from the first kick until the last. A warrior doesn't save himself. If he does he will be defeated, may just die. Look at me. I'm more exhausted than any of you. For the last fifteen minutes of the hell we just went through I ran on empty. All I had left was heart. I couldn't kick worth a damn. My form would have been an embarrassment to most black-belts in other schools. But *Kokorokan* isn't about form. It's the way of the heart. A black-belt gives his all at the beginning, and when that is gone, he has only his heart to keep him going. And that is how he survives. That is his victory."

Without thought the man's consciousness opened to the truth of *sempai* Martone's telling. No emptiness remained within him. His heart beat strong.

HIS WORDS SPOKEN, the *sempai* turned to his locker, stripped and trudged silent and barefooted to the shower. No one dared follow. The others mumbled among themselves, pulled clean clothes over sweaty bodies, and slunk away. But I sat a moment longer before rising and striding out into the crisp new night. I was committed to the black-belt's path. The way of the heart opened clear before me. I would risk all, would give all, and in that way my emptiness would become full.

Throughout the course of this section I have come to call the *shodan* who spoke so as *sempai*, a term in the traditional form usually reserved for *sandans*, third degree black belts. At the time in *Sensei* Hoffman's *dojo*, other than *sensei* Hoffman himself, there was only one other black-belt, Patrick Martone, and thus, as the very senior student, the honorific *sempai* was used with his name. He was known to the man then as *Sempai Martone*, and now, as *Sensei*. It takes nine years minimum to advance from *shodan* to *sensei*, but, in truth, from the day of his first thousand kick class, the man knew that *sempai* Martone was a true and valuable teacher. For the first time he not only gave voice to something the man's father had often tried and just as often failed to instill in him, but also gave it substance. The man's father had somehow, perhaps genetically, bequeathed him the heart of which he as well as *sempai*

Martone spoke, but that sweaty, first-degree, fresh from senior-brown, black-belt, as he trod away beaten but undefeated, stamped the awareness of what "heart," not strength, not courage, not perseverance, not victory, was. Not what it meant, but what it was, how it existed, had always existed, within him, forever upon his dark and mysterious soul as well as upon the sun-swept surface of his consciousness. The man, while remaining himself, became someone more as well.

A period of introspection followed for many days. *Karate* became his obsession. *Sempai* Martone and *Sensei* Hoffman taught his body and mind, allowed his heart to expand itself into every aspect of his every endeavor. The man began to think with more than his mind, to believe beyond the boundaries of faith. *Sensei* Hoffman, it turned out, had an interesting favorite expression for those in obvious difficulty. "Pain is like candy," he would laugh. "It's sweet, and you can never get enough."

The man loved that.

As his skill level grew and his belts became dirtier and dirtier wearing into brown and, he hoped, eventually black, the man found himself the first-time father of a second family, dweller within a newly-purchased house of endless possibilities, and, as a result he consciously rededicated himself to his five lifetime priorities: Family, Friends, HVCC, Motorcycle, and *Karate*. He also developed a sense of being always in the process of becoming. Becoming a black-belt he thought, an elevated and enlightened being such as the Chinese systems had promised yet had failed to deliver. He knew beyond doubtful shadows that he would achieve transcendence, would in hard rather than soft fashion become an essential peaceful warrior, peaceful due to his invulnerability to mere human assault. Yes, he began to envision himself as more than Bruce Lee, *Kaicho* Nakamura, or *Shihan* Rossetti. He knew that on his own he had no chance. But he more than merely felt that something as yet unrevealed to him was about to lift him above and beyond his current limited state. He simply had to train, had to wait.

Part of the process was class twice a week in a small room in a factory in Green Island where he and a group of working men went at the discipline, the art of *Karate* with a ferocity not found in the other settings. Soon Derek joined, and soon thereafter the man discovered he had already lifted himself out, had risen above. He would never become Bruce Lee however.

Derek, a former Catholic, husband and father of two children, had graduated from a Baptist seminary, was the Youth Pastor of the nondenominational Loudonville Community Church, was two degrees ahead of the man in *Karate* and soon became the man's fast friend. They sweated, sparred, and supported each other during class and found common ground for discussion outside. At times they traveled to other *dojos* in the organization, and it was during one of those that the man found his elevation.

As one might expect, as they drove, the conversation usually turned to religious matters, and the man was reminded of the recent past, when over two years' time he had entertained himself in conversation with a Jehovah's Witness until the evangel abandoned all hope of conversion and somewhat bitterly gave up the attempt. The man had been bitter also, bitterly disappointed; he dearly loved discussions with people who knew more than did he about such things as Physics and Religion. The witness' name had also been Derek.

Karate Derek seemed equally committed to his beliefs and equally as fluent in the language of Scripture and Faith. Also at the core of his repertoire dwelt a deep strain of something the man had perhaps been subconsciously denying in himself ever since Nan's House and Billy Graham. Karate Derek saw Jesus the Christ as his Personal Savior. He was a Born Again Christian.

As one might expect, the topics of conversation between the two of them drifted from the multitudinous natures of the various

Judeo/Christian/Islamic institutions, beliefs, and practices into areas of more a personal context. Derek was not pushy in his belief at all, in fact might have been considered by some of his more evangelical colleagues as lacking the appropriate amount of zeal. He listened as well as spoke and possessed a sensitivity toward areas wherein the man exhibited reticence, thus allowing the man opportunity to steer their conversations around such areas as his own personal beliefs beyond the vague assertion that his study of the philosophies behind the martial arts had instilled within him a deep respect for the Zen/Taoist world view, his trump card being, "Every way is the way." He was well aware that Jesus had assigned "The Way" to himself and could tell that Derek was unconvinced, but was impressed by the other man's ability to express disapproval without offering even the mildest of judgments. Derek, it seemed, was a true Christian Gentleman.

One afternoon, perhaps the end result of the workings of God, perhaps simply the arrival of the Preacher's first opening, as the man happily wrapped himself around a post-workout fish fry, he saw fit to mention to Derek the case of a former in-law who had turned Christian and who had invited him to a tent revival/faith-healing meeting.

If Derek responded too quickly, the man never noticed. Ted's sauce is just too good to allow one to abandon its spell for such trivialities. And so, without any real thought beyond slurping up a spicy dribble from off his lower lip, the man responded honestly to Derek's question. "Yes," he spat beyond deep-fried flakes, "I have been to a revival...that is if TV counts."

And with absolutely no sense of danger and unaware that Derek's own fry lay unattended in his lap, answered the follow-up. "Billy Graham. It was at Pam's grandmother's."

"Yea. I saw that part. Those folks really get into it. Crying. I think some even might of passed out."

For some reason at that point the sauce lost its tang, the fish its salt. He was hooked and despite himself leapt into Derek's net. "I even said the prayer, you know.... Twice. And nothing happened. Nothing. The show went off; I drank some tea, and Pam and I went back home. No offense, but far as I can see, either I'm not the kind Jesus wants or else all those others are victims of some kind of mass hysteria. Sorry, man, but that's just the way I see it."

"It doesn't matter," Derek asserted, shaking his head "No" while affirming both with tone and body a big "Yes." "You said the prayer. You mean it?"

The man thought he remembered well, and probably did. "Yes," he responded. "Both times."

"Then," the Preacher smiled, "you may not know it yet, but you have found Jesus, have welcomed him into your heart and your life. Not everybody sees fireworks, falls over or even gets the slightest rush. It's possible Jesus was with you even before you prayed. He may have been the very reason for the prayer. Anyway, he's been with you at least since that time, and he's with you now even if you don't know it. You, James, are a Born Again Christian." Then he no longer could constrain it. He laughed speckles of whitefish all over the newly, or not so newly, consecrated one.

BEFORE RETURNING HOME I stopped off at the rectory with Derek. We said a prayer together and I signed a small card affirming my faith. I also took one for Pam, prayed with her later in the evening, and we both, whether or not either of us is in the mood to assert it, and way too often we are not, became and remain Born Again followers of Jesus and believers in the miracle of his dual, human and divine, nature. Of course, at least for me such was the beginning of a spiritual quest rather than its end.

THE FOLLOWING FEW years brought more doubt, systemic

uncertainty, and thoughtless decisions. For a time, with *Sensei* Hoffman, we attended Loudonville Community Church. Eventually, because Derek moved on to a new position in a new state, we found ourselves adrift. But then came a midnight visit cloaked in dreams of my youth. I walked into the darkened interior of St. Patrick's Cathedral directly from off the sunlight Main Street of Wellsboro, Pennsylvania. There to greet me was my Creative Writing/Shakespeare/Chaucer Professor Dr. Evelyn Boyd, an Anglican. Behind her shimmered the forms of those who had climbed those steps before me. They faded in and out of perceptibility neither there nor gone. Incense softened the glow of distant candles. Voices rose in prayer.... But not to God. To me. "Come home," they whispered in voices musical with memory.

So, home I traveled, a road neither too long nor too steep. Pam and I had been married in a civil ceremony presided over by her grandfather, a retired Justice; our daughter, Moira, had been presented to the congregation at Loudonville but never baptized. Sarah neither. Within a year's time, I had secured an annulment of my first marriage from Rome and had seen my daughters baptized. Pam had converted to Catholicism, and we had remarried in the Church. Again, the end result was an unexpected beginning.

The Catholic Church is no easy mistress for one such as I, especially one who is a born again Christian, is somewhat infected with Jehovah's Witness' ideas, and who has read the Bible through in its entirety, has read the four Gospels innumerable times, and who has been greatly influenced by a prayer group peopled primarily by former Catholics who left the Church for, as they would put it, the Truth of God. Sometimes, I must confess, these people, Witnesses and the Fallen Away, as my mother would have called them, have greater claim to spirituality and God's truth than many popes, priests, bishops, and cardinals. I somehow though, still needed the Catholic Church. Soon, I came to realize that my need was due to the Eucharist. I tasted the bread and wine, the

Body and Blood, time and time again. Through the sacrament I found I could know Jesusin the same way those at the Billy Graham rally must have. No, I never fainted dead away. But I did go away quite often. And for a brief time each of those times I KNEW God.

A BRIEF DIGRESSION, indeed not a digression at all, is needed here. Pam's experience in The Rite of Christian Initiation of Adults (RCIA) altered, at least for a time, my social/spiritual course as well as hers. Through her experience and education, I became enthralled by the no longer new to others yet newly discovered by me changes in and possibilities of the post-Vatican II Roman Catholic Church. I joined a Catholic Prayer/Bible study group, brought Pam's sister to the faith, and stood as godfather to my niece. But my desire to become part of this new thing ran, if not deeper, at least beyond these. I enlisted both as an instructor in the RCIA program and as a tenth-grade Catechist in the parish Faith Formation program. Not exactly filled with missionary zeal, I, nonetheless, felt a more than urgent if less than burning desire to bring the good news to as many needy souls as possible. Thus did I embark upon another of my paths toward disillusionment, a state which just might be a necessary precursor to enlightenment.

First, most of those in RCIA seemed to be there as some minor sort of social adjustment brought about by an impending marriage, the result of a nagging parent's insistence upon a laggard offspring's need for confirmation, or, in at least one case, a friend's affirmation of some brand or other of sisterhood. Rarely, perhaps in two cases, was the candidate, whether a full-fledged catechumen or someone in need of a sacramental update, participating as a result of spiritual thirst or hunger. As has always been the case, in much of the new as always within the old Church, forms were filled out because that is what one does with forms, and procedures were followed as matters of routine. Rarely did the newly initiated show up for Mass after the Easter Vigil— that is until another formal Church ceremony such as a wedding or funeral demanded their reluctant appearance.

True awareness, however, grew slowly over the first two years of my six-year tenure in Faith Formation. Before I begin in earnest, I must state unequivocally that the majority of my public-school tenth graders were intelligent, interesting, and inquisitive young men and women. Their Catholic—religious—education had been either sorely neglected or woefully inadequate. Or both.

My first class of my first year I asked the twenty-some students who was there because he or she wanted to be. One young man raised his hand. The others simply stared. And so I began individual questioning. To the inquiry *Why are you here then?* the universal response was *Because my parents want me to get confirmed.* When asked *Do you intend to continue with your religious education after Confirmation?* one or two *Maybes* were far outnumbered by emphatic *Nos.* And finally, in response to *How many of you will continue attending Mass regularly once you are on your own?* More than fifty-percent asserted that they would not, and one brave soul quipped, "The Catholic Church can go to Hell as far as I'm concerned." The appreciative laughter accompanying this was most telling. Sadly the same scenario continued with much the same results throughout my time as a Catechist.

Sad as the preceding may be, the reason for this digression came in another area of my endeavor. May I say here that from my first childhood moment of recognizing that I was a Catholic, I also became aware that the Eucharist was the REAL Body and Blood of Jesus Christ. The term *Transubstantiation* entered my vocabulary not much later. During my tenure as a catechist I taught perhaps a hundred tenth graders, and of that number no more than a dozen had even heard of the term *transubstantiation*, only a couple had any idea what it meant, and not one of them accepted the idea as anything but ludicrous. To me, the Eucharist was and still is the soul of Catholicism; to them it was, and I must believe still is, a joke. I present their non-belief in such fashion as warning to the reader. Possibly all which has been so far related may have seemed far-fetched, but from this point on it just may appear so counterintuitive and anti-rational as to be an absurdity of like nature to the insane idea of Jesus Christ alive and waiting to be drunk and eaten disguised as a taste of wine and a chip of wholly tasteless bread.

I left Faith Formation in despair, not for the souls of my students nor for my own; rather I despair for the Catholic Church. I still attend irregularly, but, other than a study group with some old friends and every now and again a new one, I volunteer for nothing and find inspiration as well as comfort elsewhere. Except for the Eucharist that is. I state unequivocally that when I take the host in my hands and lay it upon my tongue, I still cannot chew it, and when I taste the forbidden wine of Christ's true blood, I not only know my God, but I am my God for a time eternal beyond all counting. Christ is flesh of my flesh, blood of my blood. I am one with God, the universe, all of humanity, and myself.

Make no mistake, this is no exaggeration. I know not the scientific details in any depth, but that which feeds us physically— bread and wine in this case—does become part of us physically and its energy aids in creating in us the possible manifestations of all that we may or may not become. And when you add the spiritual presence brought about at the Consecration not by the priest but by the believers, each and every one present who truly participates, even if only one or two be among the multitude, you have transformed the mundane into the divine. In other words, I and any who believe with me create within the bread and wine of communion the actual although not recognizably physical presence of Jesus Christ, the Son of God and in all respects God. We as well, at least for a limited time, hold not God within us but are ourselves trans, con or con-trans substantiated. As Heinlein suggested in *Stranger in a Strange Land*, We are God.

This is not as dementedly egotistic if not completely delusional as it may seem. First, if one accepts, as do I, that bread and wine are capable of becoming body and blood, that they are not just symbols, but are the actual and living body and blood of Jesus Christ, a man long dead, then it is not even the smallest of steps but simply an effortless segue into realizing that the human individual may also be so transformed. It must be remembered at this point that the bread and wine are quickly subsumed into the substance and energy systems of the individual communicant and thus quickly pass from separate and individual existence. So too, often before returning to his pew, is the communicant effortlessly digested into the demanding body of society, providing her substance and essential energy to the larger bodies called family, community, genus and species. All too quickly we repress our awareness of the divinity we have so briefly known ourselves to be.

Perhaps the prime reason for this almost instantaneous reseparation is our innate human reluctance to be other than that which we naturally and phenomenologically are. Another equally important cause, however, just may be the fact that even the truest believer knows that to be Jesus, to be God upon this earth, is to be forever separate, never again to experience the always safe, secure, and comforting pleasures of thoughtless materialism, of blind commitment to human purposes, to the undiluted love of parent for child or lover for beloved. Jesus always found himself saying things like, "Think not that I am come to send peace on earth: I come not to send peace, but a sword. For I have come to turn a man against his father, a daughter against her mother.... Anyone who loves father or mother more than me is not worthy of me; anyone who loves son or daughter more than me is not worthy of me" (Matthew: 10:34-36).

The moment of communion, however, actual communion

that is, not the mere receiving of the sacrament so many reduce it to, is not easily forgotten, and, not in my case alone, exists as a longing not easily denied, a desire so profoundly spiritual as to become over time an obsessive physical demand as well. Unity with the divine possibilities of one's humanity is never completely forgotten. The participant in this unification is forever changed, altered in an immutable fashion so that he or she can never again experience the innocence of the sacrificial lamb who delights in life right up to the moment of slaughter; if I were to propose a definition of Nietzsche's *Ubermensch* I would point to myself and other like spirits on their way away from the communion rail and twist Hopkins' line just a bit more. *That is the life we all were born for as well as the blight we still must mourn for.*

Jesus also made many hopeful pronouncements and has provided his lambs with beatitudes and sermons on mounts to reinforce their careless ideas of following the ethic proclaimed by Catholicism as well as by the other major world religions. They do not, however, partake of the true freedom of those individuals for whom "Take up your cross..." (Mark: 8: 34-35) has become the tragic message of the entire experience. Whatever we do, Lamb, Wolf, Fatted Calf or Tyger, we all will die. Always must come The End.

I STAND BEHIND Pam who stands in the Communion line at St. Mary's Church across from Washington Park in Troy. The season is spring. The time is Lent, and we have been attending Mass every day. This day, two old people up from us, a mysterious one waits. She is dark and always clad in a fashion Pam finds fascinating, having named her in our awareness, the Anne Rice Woman. I know for a fact that she is neither the author nor is she one of that most imaginative creator's supernatural beings. She is, however, a mystery, at least to the casual observer.

It is Anne's turn to receive. She kneels and holds out her

tongue. The floor is dusty with springtide dried mud. Her knees are bare. The priest, an old man, must bend to her. One can see that he does so with some degree of discomfort as well as, perhaps, another point or two of resentment. None of us in line so much as cough. Our wonder, however, glitters in the stained illumination. What's with this Anne anyway? Why can't she just hold out her hands and move on? We've got places to go and things to do.

As much as I enjoy sharing the Anne Rice persona with Pam, we both know the woman's true name. It is not Anne. She is a very devout and conservative Catholic and is active in promoting her vision of Holy Mother Church, its Magisterial teachings, and the proper liturgical practices. As well, she espouses a special devotion to the Virgin Mary. But most of all, she is passionately devoted to the Eucharist, the precious body and blood of Our Lord Jesus Christ.

She passes the wine by as I know she will and retreats to the rear of the old church where in a great pool of sunlight she kneels at prayer, an agony of transcendence melting the age from her face and freeing from within an illumination for a time warmer than the sun's.

The cover of this book bears a reproduction of one of Bartolome Esteban Murillo's *Dolorosa* paintings. This particular sorrowful mother could be Anne's own mother, could, in fact, be Anne. The Madonna is plain, her garments loose, her form bordering upon the awkward, while from within her radiates a sense of expectancy, the sure and certain hope of God's grace...or possibly another disappointment, another heaping of sorrow. Anne's form, her face, her more modern garments, save for her black-lace *mantilla*, her bare arms, hands clasped before her in prayer all convey the same message. It is not hope, not resignation, acceptance, anger or denial. It is love in the face of cruelty, tragic courage and resistance right up to and beyond the disappearance of all she holds dear, so much more unspeakable than the mere termination of her own insignificant existence. She, like the Murillo, is Everywoman—and man as well. And yet....

She is transfigured. She too is God. She too is beyond all the sorrow, all the pain. She cannot know defeat. She will always overcome.

At least for a time. I watch as the sun dims behind an invisible cloud and the light fades back within her. She quickly finds her keys, stands at the appropriate time, blesses herself, casts a quick smile our way and is off. Our Lady of Sorrows too has much to do.

CHAPTER FIVE

George and the Doctors

I AM ABLE to state unequivocally that I do not simply believe in God: I LOVE God. My Father. As a young man, for the time I was simple enough to allow it, my biological father and I traveled many miles together, enjoying some times nearly idyllic and others no doubt well into the realm of total dysfunction. As I have stated previously, Pa taught me to drive when I was twelve. He would drive us out of range of my mother and the local law then turn the wheel over to me and all around the county we would go. Sometimes just for the pure pleasure of wind and rain, sun and shadow. Sometimes as time of instruction on snow-treacherous highways, sometimes as an escape from the boredom of small-town, reluctantly sober existence. We each knew there was something more, and sometimes we thought an old Chevy or a new Cadillac could take us there. And sometimes, that almost happened. Sometimes, I swear it did.

A long moment ago, while yet merely upon the brink of knowledge, I wrote the following. It speaks to the longing of my soul at the time for a moment lost when we, my father and I, were able to reach that place.

My father took me drivin'
Him, the big blue Buick
And his rough voice laughin'

To a hilltop place where two roads cross.

And we threw stones at poles
And walked the awkward fields
Two barren, lonely souls
Unable to keep pace

In a hilltop place where two roads cross

The summer sun shone dry
And golden for someone
Else. Our words of goodbye
Unspoken as our tears

In a hilltop place where two roads cross

Once more again alone
With him a memory
His smilin' eyes all gone
I face the dry, sad sunlight

Of a hilltop place where two roads cross

The very specific hilltop place to which the poem refers is in
Pennsylvania about five miles outside of Wellsboro and up the hill
to a crossroads. Three of the corner lots are two hay fields and a
pasture; the other is a cemetery. A friend, my wife Maureen, and I
used to drive there on certain warm nights when we had not
sufficient money for a bar but were able to buy enough quarts of
Schmidt's to move us away for a moment from the desperate
future we saw revealing itself before us. One of the gravesites was
that of a child. Always would we pour out a libation for him and
invite him—had he lived he would have been about our age—to
join in our companionship. My father was still alive, but in
memory of the two of us as once we had been, I would cast a

stone or two across the dirt road at one of the posts beginning to fail their original purpose, no doubt inadequate to the task of remaining steadfast in the face of their irrelevancy. No more cattle grazed there. The distant barns were tumbling in upon themselves, and the crossroads had, it seems, been abandoned to the ghosts of a time well past. To drinkers and to dreamers as well.

AT ONE TIME in a time well gone, as I stood shivering from the ice cream soda I had just consumed far too quickly, my father held conversation with someone I did not recognize, a working-man by his clothes and the language he employed. A displaced coal miner it turned out. My father was to me and I believe to most others, possibly even my mother, a man most mysterious. For instance, he often bragged that while in college he had run for a touchdown with a broken leg. We, my brothers and sister, uncles and aunts, scoffed. Only upon his death did we discover the newspaper clipping he had saved, detailing that very feat. Another of his supposed tall tales was of his political career. He claimed to have once held Grace Kelly on his lap while meeting with her father as well as the future governor of Pennsylvania, Dave Lawrence. Behold, after he died we found a picture and a note from Jack Kelly himself. All would attest to his being head of the WPA for Northern Pennsylvania, but he also claimed to have been significantly influential as Democratic County Chairman and dispenser of "favors" to all and sundry.

The man on the street corner seemed to confirm this. He spoke tragically of a place called Antrim and the passing of the good old days when my father ran things and how the new guy was a worthless sack of something I was not allowed to say. And he did seriously request that my father consider returning to politics. These things are the stuff of renewed visions of glory and so Pa spoke to Ma. She said "No," and nothing more transpired. At the time I thought she was just plain mean and unable to, as they say, "reach for the brass ring." Little was I aware that the ring comes at a cost; the carousel and its wooden horses, round and round, up and down all day, take one nowhere and the brass ring just assures another ride.

Anyway, the stranger's mention of Antrim spoke to my preteen soul. It was named after an Irish town and had planted a bit of the Auld Sod in Tioga County. I had never been to either of the Antrims. I longed to someday visit both. One of the roads of that place upon the hill led directly to the fabled Borough. Sadly, we still never ventured along that way, and eventually Maureen, Erin and I moved to Troy. I had never gone to Antrim.

MY FATHER LIES buried alongside my mother in Stephentown, New York. One of my brothers and his wife occasionally tend to the grave. Most of us are too fractured from the dead as well as from the living to care. I last visited the site ten years ago and, thanks to Pam's influence, left some flowers. Since then neither of us has returned, and, I would guess, she too has come to realize that a gravesite is a mere repository of things no more than incidental to the loved one now gone. With this in mind, in 2008 I introduced Pam and Moira and Sarah to the spot where my father's memory most lives and where his spirit—should spirits care about such trivialities—sometimes still visits. The hilltop place.

The kids were impressed by the child's grave and my stories of intoxicated nights and the first dawn of Beatlemania. Pam was less than impressed, finding empathy for the mother who may have come upon her son's grave littered with empty bottles. I would have preferred "decorated" to "littered," but Pam does have her ways. She, however, was touched by the memories of my father and suggested we drive on down the road and make my first visit to the fabled town of Antrim. I was no longer able to toast the child with a beer, but I did, however, tip a bottled water his way, and, after tossing a few stones at the broken posts, Pam having great success with her aim, we set off for the sacred precincts. The drive was beautiful, wildlife abundant and the kids, normally way too easily bored with their parents' obsessions and frivolous Odysseys, were content to count dead animals—fox, skunk, two opossums and one deer—along our brief way.

Antrim was a sad fulfillment of all my expectations. A bar still lit its windows with red and green neon, the street was paved, but only six or seven back-woods, redneck homes were occupied. The overwhelming presence was that of Damage Control. I know not the processes, but the old mines must have been mighty polluters and modern technology had been lifted into place in order to minimize the damage they once had done and still threatened to inflict. We followed the lane to its dead end. A cemetery. And there I saw it. From times long gone, a friend. My friend Jim's headstone blazed from the tailing field, the newest structure in all of Antrim, Pennsylvania. He had lived with Maureen and me for a time during our college years, had once found two rats in the crib of his new baby, had been divorced, had reestablished himself, remarried, and moved on. Had died.

Just to reinforce the moment, I followed our road back past the crossroad hilltop and down into the valley of Wellsboro. Just as I remembered, spread out upon the flatland at the foot of the hill sprawled Broad Acres nursing home. From death to old age, what are our choices? One of my brothers and my sister were born in Soldiers and Sailors Memorial Hospital in Wellsboro, as was my first daughter Erin. We are all out of there now, but wherever we go, our options are but two: Live to be old and then die or die young. Do we have a choice? Is one preferable to the other? More natural? Or bearable? Perhaps, perhaps not, but any way you assess our predicament we lose. Fate? Free Will? Who can actually care? It all ends the same.

I HAVE PURPOSEFULLY been concealing something for quite some number of pages now. Like unto Martha McInroy Slattery I too have heard the voice of the One I choose to call God on several occasions after the reproduction room. I cannot say how many such visitations my mother failed to share with us. Possibly none. But I cannot help but wonder if, like me, she didn't hear some things far too trivial to relate to others. She was human. She, as do most of us, must have disliked ridicule and skeptical smiles, especially from those she loved. I do not know, but I do realize that the first of my God-experiences lends itself way too easily to skepticism and mockery. By this time in my narrative, I do not care. If I desired completely to avoid such things I never would have begun this telling of my heart so close now to being ended. And so....

The three communications I feel most relevant here are as follows. The first seems the least significant. All three somehow involve my friend George, and, despite his not being a major player in any of them, he is ever present. He is too old and too much the teetotaler ever to be compared to Cousin Mike, but just like Mike he has had a direct hand in the lengthening of my life span.

He and I ran long distances together three or four times a week; our weekly mileage sometimes reached one hundred. This wore heavily upon my, at times, very overweight body. I ran two of my marathons with over 200 pounds blubbering upon my five-foot-nine frame. It should have come as no surprise then that one of my big toes began first to hurt and eventually to develop a sore which would not heal. Pam's calm suggestions and George's nagging concern eventually drove me to visit a podiatrist. He looked, X-rayed and pronounced sentence. What I suffered from was called a bunion, but no ordinary *hallux abducto-valgus*; its effect was exacerbated by a bone-spur of truly grim proportions. I needed surgery.

I would not have it. The doctor and I argued for a time, and his parting words as I exited the office were, "You're not afraid to ride that motorcycle without even modest protective gear. How can you be afraid of an operation on your big toe?"

I could have killed him, but instead allowed the door to shut him off at least from my life. I started my bike and left. But I didn't get very far. My pipes are straight, their song overpowering. Above it all, however, boomed the voice.

"Turn around," it thundered louder than my pipes, powerful enough to shake the maple trees, yet unheard except by me. I did as I was commanded, returned to the podiatrist's office and scheduled surgery for the next week in the now passed on Leonard Hospital.

The foot surgeon cut a notch in my bone, hacked off the spur, and sent me home able to run free again. Well, that is, after wearing a disgusting bandage and a plastic boot for six-weeks. I hated every bit of it with two exceptions. I continued to work out six days a week in Karate which increased my reputation in the *Dojo*. Both Pam and George thought I was crazy, but then who can tell a maniac that he truly is insane? The second not unbearable aspect of the surgery and six-week boot was my getting handicap parking privileges. Our *Dojo* was located in a large shopping mall, and parking was always a problem. Not for me. My permit was good for three months, and I used it well.

The preceding must seem to at least border upon the trivial, but in actuality my analysis, made several years later as I faced another surgery, has me convinced that the command to turn around amounted to God's providing me with a dry-run of upcoming attractions. I have heard it said that God never gives us more than we can handle. My own perception is that God gives us life, and among all the things life may hold are bunions. And Alzheimer's, stroke, heart attack, cancer, crucifixion, and death. We will all weep in our own gardens, but just as did Jesus, we must rise up and meet our destined end. We ask for an out. As did Christ. But, God must say "NO." Life must end for each and every one of us in death, and for most of us, along with death, comes suffering to plunge us down into the great hole of despair. Even Jesus lived that moment before he died.

And how do such rambles spring up from surgery on my big toe? Simple: God did not give me a bone-spur and a bunion. Life, running, *Karate,* unhealthy lifestyle choices, and genetic predisposition performed that task. Such predisposition was made manifest for all to recognize in the person of Jesus, Son of God and the Blessed Virgin Mary, wonderworker, teacher, and victim. To my mind no one has ever had it so good. Or so bad. God's Son who taught the Lord's Prayer to all succeeding generations gave us the gift of God as "Our Father." God was his father too. Yet, when he prayed that his loving and beloved Abba (Daddy) take the cup from him, his Father essentially told him to suck it up and get on with the job. Because he was human, Jesus naturally feared suffering and death exactly as does any of us. Again, because he was human, not in order to satisfy some blood-addled tyrant's need for a sacrifice, Jesus had to die. He was a human being. All human beings are mortal. Jesus the human being had to die. Even God could not absolve his own Son of that one.

It may seem a trifle grandiose, my comparing the Passion, Death, and Resurrection of Christ with podiatric surgery from which I recovered nicely, running faster than ever, and kicking harder. And yes way out on the fringes where metaphor dissolves into chaos I discern a certain validity to that perception. However, the core of the metaphor, its appropriateness, is due to the similarity in the cyclical nature of the two events: Life, Suffering and Prayers, Death, and Return. My life is equally as human as was that of Jesus; my suffering was minor, but it was suffering nonetheless; my garden was my desire to avoid the suffering by riding away. Jesus' "NO," and my "Turn Around," were God's commands, not to be ignored. So Jesus climbed the hill of death and I, far less burdened, accepted the surgeon's knife and bone-cutter as my fate. Afterward, did we both not reemerge from our own Hades back into the light?

I recognize that the above is a stretch, but it is valid as deep as it goes, and I would venture so far as to say that we all at different times and with differing degrees of intensity experience, even should we not recognize it, the actuality of Jesus' words admonishing the disciples: "If anyone would come after me, he must deny himself and take up his cross and follow me" (Mark: 8:34-35). By living our lives, suffering our pain, feeling Death's black breath ever hotter on our necks, we follow Jesus. Much is said by theologians and preachers of the Gospel concerning the meaning of these words. Most agree that Christ was calling for something or other called "Death to Self," and that He is requiring "Absolute Surrender." As is more often than not the case, I disagree. Others will claim Jesus was speaking of the burdens we all carry from time to time or over the course of our lives. Again, I disagree.

To my mind and heart the words bring a simple comfort. If I suffer pain, so what? Even Jesus did. When I confront death, I will simply be following the example of the Man who, among many, has brought Joy to my life. And as Jesus taught us, and Bob Dylan sang, Death is not the end. Now, I do not claim that my toe put me on the same plain as the crucifixion, nor do I assert that my experience taught me anything at the time. Instead, I was left to wonder, "Why would God want me to have my foot operated on?" My answer is as I have just tried to explain. Through that little trial I was made strong enough to face greater obstacles on down the road.

One other question, however, has plagued me since the day of the toe: My mother was turned back from a train in order that she and my brother might live. In my, seemingly lesser case, was I, as I now choose to assume, turned toward rather than away from something or was there tragedy awaiting me on the road ahead and God simply moved me from harm's way? I do not know the answer and so am left to wonder if the surgery on my toe was merely a side effect of God's more significant intervention. My heart embraces this latter. God is no Cousin Mike and there was no rocket beside me. God, however, was, as he always is, there. Am I miraculously protected? My brain, however, speaks with a clearer voice. "Dry run, you fool. It was to make you strong."

THE SECOND GOD-TO-JAMES message is the most complex and in many ways the most significant of the three. George (again) and I had traveled to Tula, Russia in March of 2004. The college sent us as part of an area-wide involvement by Albany and Tula as Sister Cities under the aegis of an international attempt at greater global understanding. We were offered the opportunity by Dr. Joseph Bulmer, and the college paid all expenses. George went out of curiosity while I went for a specific reason. Tula was the home of Leo Tolstoy.

We both made friends and learned much about the Russian people and their educational system as it ranges from what we would term pre-K all the way to the university. My particular fulfillment resulted from two events. First was a visit to and a tour of Yasyana Polyana which included a walk through the birch woods to the place where Tolstoy lies buried. Along the path to the gravesite, Natasha, the more outgoing of our two translator/companions, asked if we would mind pausing for a moment and allowing Yelena, the shy one, to recite a poem she had written. So standing apart from us in her red coat amidst snow-deep woods and barren trees, the young woman spoke, first in Russian and then in English. I have no copy of her poem, and perhaps, if I had, the stark beauty of its lines, the sad prayer to no god in particular would appear overly sentimental and stereotypically young girl romantic. But, not that morning. That day, 2 April 1994, will always be with me. I picture the four of us now, flakes of snow adding meaning to the words of hope and anguish, and I see Yelena facing me across a small white clearing, her eyes brown and rich as the snow-drifted earth beneath our feet. And with the vision I remember a song from a long ago movie which touched my sentimental heart in much the same way as has Yelena's poem. "The Rose," as sung by Bette Midler ends with these lines: "Just remember in the winter/Far beneath the bitter snows/Lies the Seed that with the sun's love/In the spring becomes the rose."[7]

Another perhaps overly sentimentalized memory of Russia stands out equally. The faculty of the Institute which acted as our host treated us to a going away lunch on the campus. They sang songs, drank beer, wine, Champagne, and, of course, vodka. As well, they read from Pushkin, and, I who do not drink, fell under the spell of some substance too powerful to explain even to myself; it was beauty; it was music; it was joy. Since then, especially in the darkness of some time, I remember the women's faces, their shy smiles afterward, and the certainty that somehow good would outlast the evil. And I remember the tank, a WWII KV1 or 2 on a concrete pad at the edge of the campus facing west. "That," said Natasha "marks the furthest advance of Hitler's forces in the region." The Nazi's were held off by some regular troops and by mobilized faculty and staff. As a result, to this day the people in that school and in that city know, perhaps from the first dawning of each individual consciousness, the true nature of life and death in a way such as a teenage fool in this country learns it only when faced with his own head-on graduation into nothingness.

MY FAVORITE IMAGINING of Tolstoy involves his sitting in his study looking through a window upon the autumn countryside. Wrapped in the futility and profound emptiness of his own existence, he observes peasants traveling from one field to the next during harvest time. Their children, swirls of dried leaves, wrap themselves around the laborers; the men and women smile and laugh, but above all they sing. Their songs are of hope and faith, but most ineluctably they express a joy beyond human understanding. Each and every one of them is both Ivan and Gerasim. Tolstoy knows that he too is Ivan but that he must become the peasant as well. He realizes that as Ivan he has believed in nothing, has valued nothing, and is himself Nothing. The inescapable fact is that the workers are happy, despite the horror of their existence. They know something he, their master, is blind to. He must discover its nature. He does exactly that.

And then moves beyond.

I HAVE LEARNED much from Tolstoy. Natasha, Yelena, and the faculty at the Tula Institute are not peasants, but from their poetry and songs, their gifts, the inexpressible beauty of their souls I have learned a lesson similar to the great writer's. Within the human being dwells a spirit as holy as any ever proclaimed by the Catholic Church. And like Ivan, I can find Joy in the tears of a child, the stoic goodness of a common man. In memory I am able still to see into the sad yet vibrant eyes of those Russian women, as they sing and read the poetry of their hearts, and therein I find the true nature of God. Behind those eyes and the eyes of all our brothers and sisters throughout the world God is ever creating and recreating himself in our image so that we may eventually see the beauty of his own mirrored by ourselves.

Although these above are not the spoken words of God, I firmly believe they are of God and from God. My time in Russia, at least to some degree, was my personal climb up the mountain toward a vision Yelena and the women, perhaps unconsciously, had shared. However, an empty feeling remained; I had been provided no specifics, shown no path to follow, no next step to take. I had not discovered the mythical "green stick." There was more. That I knew. But was it buried back in Russia?

I had to return.

As I by that time had come to expect, when obstacles such as an almost immediate return to Russia would involve loomed above and before me, God seemed to move the mountains aside. An invitation arrived from Tula. The two of us, George and I, were invited to a symposium to be held early in September, 1995. Dr. Bulmer was supportive and offered us another all expenses paid trip. We readily accepted and my course was made level and smooth back to the land of impossible sadness and beauty. Again I would lose myself in those women's eyes, their poetry and song once more lifting me out of myself and into the spirit land where such tragic beauty dwells. Or so I surmised.

My guess is that God had no hand in the invitation or our being sponsored by the college. As is necessary, I applied for a visa, and, whether due to my own error or to a mix-up at the Russian Consulate, it came back with incorrect dates. I would be required either to apply for a new visa (the remaining time was too short) or hope no one looked too closely at my documents. I was willing to take the chance—I still thought that God had ordained the journey and that, as most fundamentalists, such as I was at the time, believe, he would provide. In fact, in the reproduction room He had as much as said so. Interesting how one thinking himself so blessed, so absolutely close to God as to be on speaking terms with him, can be so deaf and blind.

The very next day after receiving the incorrect visa, I was informed that the originally booked flight had been changed and that instead of flying directly to Moscow we would first land in Helsinki where we would take another airline to Russia.

God's spoken word was once again short and imperious. "Don't go," He commanded.

I have always been more superstitious than is average, and the altered flight plans might have convinced me to bow out, but I doubt it. I have always been one to ignore such negatives as fear and pain. Except for God's voice, I would not have wimped out. But He spoke as I sat alone, my thoughts gone random, the Doors on my stereo: *Riders on the Storm*. I was not to ride anywhere that August except around town. The journey to Tolstoy, the heavenly women, and spiritual epiphany was not to be. I walked into my Dean's office and informed him that the signs were truly omens and that I could not go as planned. He, acknowledging his own superstitious nature, wholeheartedly agreed. George went without incident. I have no doubt that had I been along there still would have been no cataclysm. God had no need to save me. He did, however, have a new highway for me to travel, and that road never left Troy, NY.

Pam and I had been married August 13 of that same year, and, to be truthful, our being newlyweds had nothing to do with at least my conscious decision to stay at home. As I reflect, however, I can see that our being married was an inextricable element in the larger unfolding of Destiny's highway. At this time I am not certain to where the road leads, but I am able to see somewhat into my future as a result of the pattern of my previous travels.

Our first daughter, Moira, was born May 12, 1996, a full month premature. I have no intention of relating the details of Pam's and my intimate life together, but to the best of her doctor's, her nurse-midwife's, and her own calculations, Moira was conceived during the time I would have been in Russia. The timing is undeniable. Thus I affirm, God had no need to save me; his purpose was to create a new life and in so doing heap joy and blessing upon us.

I am no modern man. Pam had a natural delivery, and I managed to stay with her until things got serious, at which point I beat a hasty retreat leaving the field to the women. In a relatively short time Pam's sister came out to tell me it was all over and that the child was a girl. An innocent, I went back into the birthing room. Pam, stoic as always, had, I was told, not so much as allowed a groan to escape during the process and was actually laughing over something one of the nurses had said. Another nurse and the midwife were engaged in some particularly bloody business. Quickly I turned back.

"Jim, don't you want to see the baby?" Sally, Pam's stepmother called. "She's over here."

Turning back to the sound, I found the same inspiration I had experienced so long ago in Tula. In the space between the gowned bodies of Sally and another nurse a tiny hand emerged from its nest of blankets. I swear it waved "Hello." And at that moment, I fell through into light. I had been born in 1941, again in 1989. As Ivan felt the resistless force pushing him toward the light, as he died, I was pulled closer to the heart of that from whence the light is born. Ivan only found life through death. May 12, 1996 I was reborn for the third time. I could never be the same. Within the Grail of my memory that hand ever beckons.

THE THIRD GOD-JAMES interaction followed hard upon a series of conversations with George concerning religion, faith, the nature of God Him/Her/Itself. I am unable to speak to George's currently held views, but at the time he consistently and coherently argued that one, an intelligent and enlightened human being such as he assumed us both to be, must find the Bible, religious dogma of all kinds, and the concept of a personal god of any sort laughable, and that only the weak, lazy, mindless, uneducated, and/or desperate are ensnared by such obvious falsehood and foolishness. These conversations occurred over the course of a week, and at the end of the last one, as we ran along a wooded lane, he pointed to a blue heron just rising in flight from a pond and swept his arm upward and outward in a graceful arc encompassing the bird, the pond, meadow and far-off mountains. Then, tipping back his head, he uttered his own prayer of adoration. "This is my God," he exclaimed. "Everything in nature all about us is God. This is Everything. It is Life. Beauty. Death, and Decay. I believe, Mr. Slattery. I believe in the God which is Nature. Not any Trinity, my God is multifarious. He is everywhere all right, because Nature is everywhere. He is omnipotent because he is all that moves and all that creates...." And then he drew in a breath, sprinted a bit ahead, and, turning to me, running backwards up the slope, he smiled, laughing out the words, "Omniscient? I don't know about that one, Mr. Slattery. Maybe only the Shadow knows," at which point he turned and sprinted the last half-mile to our cars, leaving me far, far behind.

The next day, a bright May afternoon, I stood over the sleeping forms of Pam and our new-born daughter Moira as they snuggled beneath the comfort of a grandmother's quilt, every bit as wondrous as any Madonna and Child could ever be. And I was struck by an awareness as powerful and absolute as the first bright moment of Creation. George was right. I stood frozen in amazement at the simple, the quotidian, and yet ineffably profound presence of Mother and Child. No wonder Joseph always seems locked out of the whole Christ thing. Life, new, brilliant, divine, and human, belongs exclusively to mother and child. I had never felt so much the outsider. The existential alienation I had always pretended at was revealed as mere intellectual snobbery. Before me, curled upon and within each other, Pam and Moira shared as one the secret of all things. Revealed through them the god that was Nature mocked my pathetic Christianity.

Feeling every bit the fool George had been trying to convince me that I must be, my mind mocked my ridiculous superstition. "Father, Son, and Holy Ghost. What an asshole...."

Before my anger and resentment could grow, however, came

the voice. Sharp and to the quick, "**Don't you stab me in the back**." It was the voice from the reproduction room, but louder, more powerful and dangerous. It was Jesus, God, and Holy Spirit.

And so....

Pam, Moira, and later Sarah are miraculous creatures, as are my first two daughters, Erin and Shannon. But then miracles come from God. As does Nature. I thank you, Jesus, every day for your admonition. And I thank you, God, for the wonder, for the joy you have given me.

AS A CHILD I was taught that God was beyond human understanding and that all attempts to comprehend Him other than through the truth as revealed to the Church fathers by the Holy Spirit were doomed to failure and possibly would lead the foolish seeker down forbidden paths into the great swamp of error, heresy, sin, and eventual damnation. God, my teachers decreed, was a mystery as were many of the teachings of the Church, and the only sure and righteous course was to submit to the authority of the Pope, the Cardinals, Bishops, and Priests, God's designated representative here on Earth who spoke for God Himself.

It is upon this rock that my Ship of Faith had foundered. The words of George concerning the god of all Nature contained more probability of truthfulness than did Catholic dogma, Magisterial pronouncements, and Biblical exegesis, some of which seemed so simple-minded as to be nothing more than childish magical thinking indulged in by fools of limited imagination. Two insights, one provided by the great Dostoyevsky in his parable of the Grand Inquisitor and the other the result of my direct experience led me to have seriously doubted any Christian church or theology well before my conversations with George. I must strongly assert here that these doubts would most assuredly have led me back into agnosticism if not perfect atheism were it not for the voice of

God that day as I gazed in wonder upon Pam's and my own Nativity scene.

But God spoke, and I heard. I am inclined to say that then and there, although, again, I was unaware of the larger picture, I experienced, cataclysmic as any Billy Graham soul-quake could ever be, an event most generally referred to as being "Born again of the Spirit." Without ever once fainting dead away and never shouting *Hallelujah,* I plunged happily ignorant into my own *Pentecost.*

MIGUEL DE UNAMUNO writes in his *Tragic Sense of Life* that "Some believe in science and in study, while others believe in the person, in inspiration, and even in ignorance." He continues with, "Rationalists seek definition and believe in the concept, while vitalists seek inspiration...."[8] It is directly in the middle of these conflicting impulses that I have found my rational yet mystical self. As time unfolds its shadows around me, I have grown to understand my situation. I will never be capable of discarding my rationality even should I wish wholeheartedly to become the cosmic madman, the eternal fool. I will always harbor doubt. My mind demands it. I will always listen to George. Thank, you God, for speaking to me as well. Your voice is real; your words are not misinterpreted psychological impulses. You speak English to me. I will not stab you in the back.

The oft quoted prayer, "Lord, I believe; help thou mine unbelief" (Mark 9:24), speaks directly to my spiritual/rational conflict. I am a recovering alcoholic who needed AA to get sober and who needs a Higher Power to maintain that condition. I am also a recovering atheist who knows that his default position is death and who, much as he abandoned after time the rooms of AA, must abandon those rooms where "Two or more gather in his name" (Mark: 9:24). AA and the Christian church worked miracles upon my body, mind, and soul. But I am once more alone and must remain so in order to do the things I must do and reach the unknown destination at the end of my mortal way. I owe a debt though to both communities. Thank you, AA and Christianity, for teaching me the fundamentals—how to walk sober and with my Higher Power. Thank you again, AA and Christianity, for opening my heart, mind, and soul to the NECESSITY, each and every new day in its own time, of following in one way or another (My way?) the second, third, and eleventh steps as Alcoholics Anonymous offers them and as basic Christianity teaches:

I *(2) came to believe that a power greater than myself could restore me to sanity, (3) made a decision to turn my will and my life over to the care of God as I understand Him,* and *(11) sought through prayer and meditation to improve my conscious contact with God as I understand Him, praying only for knowledge of His will for me and the power to carry that out.*[9]

I have prayed the *Lord's Prayer* daily ever since the meeting when the fragile woman held my hand even though it hurt her to do so. That moment is the first, and to the best of my awareness, the only instance of my adult life when another human spirit joined in prayer with my own, when another human spirit gave of its own waning energy so that I might grow strong. I do not know the woman's name nor do I know of her fate. She may have been a passing angel, but I think not. Her very mortal faith and hope, the charity which dwelt within her, despite the agony which boiled all about her, for a brief second which I believe will last for all eternity, opened my heart in spite of my mind to both the tragedy of human existence and the beauty of its expression in each and every one of us who are lucky enough to be God's children.

All for me, however, becomes always too complex. Despite the KISS admonition echoing within so many AA rooms, I continue on my intricate and deceptively branching path. At the time of my conversations with George a major stumbling block to my simple acceptance of God was the concept of the Trinity. The prayers of my youth, recitations of the Rosary and penances in particular were occasions of multiple repetitions of the following:

Glory be to the Father
And to the Son
And to the Holy Spirit
As it was in the beginning
Is now and ever shall be
World without end.

Instead of any sort of devotion or certainty concerning the nature of God, this prayer increased my confusion and aided me along my way to non-belief. What an absolutely foolish, anti-rational, notion the trinity is. Three separate persons, each God and all of them God. If God is the Father, how can he be the Son as well? If God has a Spirit, how is that Spirit both His and not His, and why does the Roman church decree that the Spirit proceeds from the Father and the Son while the Orthodox claims from the Father only? And, above all, how can the Spirit "proceed from" either or both yet be an entity at the same time together with and separate from them? In other words, how can God be three equal "persons" and yet One God? And finally, if God is three "persons" how is it that the Spirit seems to be a dove or tongues of flame but never a person at all? In truth, while I was meditating upon the sleeping forms of my wife and daughter, another of Murillo's paintings, this one depicting Madonna and Child Jesus whose tender hand, much like my own Moira's, rests gently upon his mother's breast, ventured into my thoughts and, but for the voice of God, the simple beauty of the renditions, both actual and artistic might have precipitated a more than temporary retreat from religious belief. Nature requires no conscious suspension of one's rationality as does a triune god. Mother is Mother. Child is Child, even should the child be Jesus. As the song goes, "It's all too beautiful," and no more need be said.

Had Jesus, Father, or Spirit, having warned me, once again become mute, I no doubt would have eventually found the futility of making logical sense of the complexity of God as Christians misunderstand him enough to put the dagger of non-belief back in my hand. Easily and most profoundly could I have embraced and rejoiced in the simple, understandable beauty of my girls, the sun rising and setting, the winter's night of mid-January, the blazing stars cold in the ice-black sky.... Nature can so easily become one's god.

But my Savior is too clever to allow that. In no time or possibly a month I "just happened" to return to rereading one of my favorite philosophers. I sometimes forget how terribly Christian his writing is, but have always been attracted to his tragic view of human life. Miguel De Unamuno has written some words which are able to draw nourishment from the wasteland and from which springs a fertile oasis of belief in God. Of particular significance at the time was his idea that we, humans, create God in our own image, and that this is the true image of God, brought about by our own faith which is in God and is also created by God, and thus is God continually creating Himself in us.[10] More simply put: God creates Faith and thus the object of that faith is the result of God's creation; thereby it is a true image of God as he reveals himself in the image and likeness of humankind, and we, in turn, are also created in the image and likeness of God.

No trinity exists in that vision, however. I was taught as a child that God created us in his image and likeness, but we are not triune. I had never come to a satisfactory accommodation with the idea, but that day I knew it was incumbent upon me to do so. But how? No book exists anywhere to explain the Trinity to my satisfaction, neither is there a cleric or theologian. Does God, however, expect me to accept it anyway? Against all reason? Contrary even to childish common sense? The answer I knew then and I know now is "Yes." But how? Drive myself down again to the edge of the abyss, leap over the side and hope that one of the Three will save me from total insanity? Does any possible way to reconcile my intelligence with God's absurdity exist — anywhere? I did not think so then and am not absolutely certain now. So what to do?

Contrary to conventional perceptions of the spiritual quest, I turned to physics for answers or at least suggested pathways to understanding. For quantum physicists one possible way of dealing with such matters as Einstein's 'spooky actions at a distance,' is to ignore them. Niels Bohr's and Werner Heisenberg's Copenhagen Solution suggests treating quantum mechanics pragmatically by ignoring the mysteries and enigmas since, for all practical purposes (FAPP), the macro-reality with which we all deal seems not to be affected in any substantial fashion by the counterintuitive quantum strangeness of the micro-universe. In other words, go with what works. In the case of the physicist this simply means proceed as though the world of classical physics were the *real* world and that the knottier problems of quantum mechanics do not exist.

As is often dictated to students of physics, "Shut up and calculate." This attitude leaves investigation of such enigmas as the double slit experiment, wave/particle duality, and non-locality to writers of science fiction and philosophers. Indeed, such ideas as the holographic universe and many worlds theory do, at first, seem far-fetched. The Copenhagen Solution, however, goes too far in the other direction, denying as it seems to do that wave-function is anything more than a useful theoretical concept and that it serves merely as a mathematical tool. Also Copenhagen suggests through the Correspondence principle that quantum descriptions of large systems closely relate to classical ones. In other words, "Ignore strange contradictions of conventional perception and logic such as Einstein's "Spooky actions at a distance," forget the absurdities of entangled particulate behavior. Shut up and calculate."

This I cannot do. Instead I embrace the great universe of possibility, and ask myself, *Cannot God be as is a mere particle of matter? Is not the spirit of God entangled with the spirit of the Human*

Entity?

I am not a writer of science fiction nor am I a philosopher. Neither am I a physicist, but I for some time have been obsessed with quantum mechanics, particularly quantum strangeness. Upon first viewing Dr. Quantum's (Fred Alan Wolf's) on-line demonstration and explanation of the classic double slit experiment, I began to intuit the true, even more complex than triune, nature of God.

This awareness of the divine nature is not to be found in any of the popular or academic dissertations on the subject. It has been formed and informed by both influences, but is particularly my own. If others find relevance to their own thoughts and understanding, so be it, and welcome to the incredible world of the spirit, both of God and humanity.

At the heart of this awareness is the profoundly simple reality of wave-particle duality and the role of the observer in creating the manifestation of the specific (particle) from the general (wave). For the purposes of this discussion the God particle (apologies to CERN) is Jesus; the wave is God. As the twentieth century wore on into the twenty-first, it became clearer that not only particles but even molecules and aggregations of molecules such as *Buckyballs* exhibited this dual nature. In other words, the universe around us is sometimes real and sometimes not—at least in any verifiable fashion. All things are matter (particle) *and* energy (wave), actuality and probability, and the observer is responsible for Probability's becoming Actuality. My perhaps heretical explanation of the Trinity rests upon this scientifically verifiable ground.

First, it must be accepted that the concept of God, however we might understand him, is the result of some basic programming within the human consciousness/brain function/imagination which is identifiable in human history over centuries and across geographical and cultural lines. As an aside, I speculate that the recent *discovery* of the so called god particle, the Higgs Boson, is a contemporary manifestation of this very essential search for something beyond ourselves. And the boson very clearly meshes with more basic approaches to God such as Trinitarianism.

If that we all have some unexplainable urge toward a higher order of being is accepted at face value, then everything else can be hung upon two pivotal points. One, one must be willing to go beyond the mundane and accept the fact that "There are more things in heaven and earth, Horatio,/Than are dreamt of in your philosophy" (Hamlet Act I, scene 5), and two, he/she must recognize the innate validity of quantum mechanics in general and specifically the reality of wave-particle duality, in other words accept that the spiritual reality is actual and that it follows the same design principles as the material. Simply on a more elevated plane.

From this point, the understanding of the Trinity and beyond is straight and clear. God is a wave of probability possibly beyond the imaginings of even the most enlightened and spiritually adept. From the outset of eternity, call it Big Bang or as you will, God existed in his own form of wave-particle duality. John I states, "In the beginning was the Word, and the Word was with God, and the Word was God/ The same was in the beginning with God" (King James). Christians consider the Word to be Jesus, as did John, but that is not the point here. God was both observer and the observed; in fact as quantum strangeness would assert, God could not manifest as anything other than probability without an observer to bring that manifestation about. That observer is appropriately called the Word, the spoken or written actuality of all the probability of thought and imagination which results in simple combinations of agreed upon symbols.

Unsolvable riddles of speculation are likely to arise from this such as did God create himself? And what does modern science offer as an answer? The Higgs Boson. So did the God Particle create both itself and everything else? As a particle—so it is scientifically identified—the boson could only be brought into existence by an observer. So was the creator of the big bang brought into existence by the void around it? Or did it, like unto God and Jesus, create its necessary observer so as to emerge into existence from its own wave of probability?

I have no answer, but I do speculate that, if one prefers to imagine the Higgs Boson as the origin of all or if another would call the Source Zeus, Chronos or Jehova it matters not to this particular seeker after truth. I call it God, but all and each of the preceding as well as innumerable others are that which we might term the Name of God. We imagine God as we are capable; we name Him as we will. He exists independent of us, however, as He was first observed both by the Word and by Himself, as does light exist in the void. He is the Wave of All Probability, and our limited observations of that wave result in our inadequate understanding and subsequent descriptions of His nature.

Thus I have arrived at my own solution to some of the knottier mysteries of the spiritual, God/Man actions and interactions. I do not fully understand the Trinity, but I will create my own FAPP accord with the concept. Father, Son, and Holy Ghost, I believe in You, I accept the mystery of your nature in its infinite state of probability, and I will carry on from there. In fact I have discovered my own symbol for you. The number: 111. 111 is itself one number, one-hundred-eleven, made up of three numbers, one, one, and one. Also $1+1+1$ equals three while $1 \times 1 \times 1$ equals one. I love it and strive to find it everywhere around me on clocks, mailboxes, and the pages of books, even license plates. God you are one and three, and I see you everywhere. In truth, I realize that I am leaping over a pile of possible doubts and objections, but like Jumpin' Jack Flash, it really is a gas.

NOT QUITE TWENTY months later another natural miracle came to pass. No way could Pam have become pregnant. But she was, and on New Year's Day, 1998 our daughter Sarah was born. Again I remained outside of the birth process. Again Pam alone bore new life into the world. My family was complete, and we were four. That evening as Sarah and her Radiant mother snuggled into weary communion, I went home and ate twenty mini-hot dogs before falling into an unnaturally troubled sleep. Into a reality other than a dream, I was awakened. "You have done well," a multi-hued bird of some tropical nature spoke against the rattle of an empty car in an empty train bound for a dead-end park in Brooklyn. I had gotten off at the last stop, the penultimate exit before the emptiness of Coney Island in the dead of winter.

CHAPTER SIX

Now I lay me down to sleep

IN THE FIFTEEN years since Sarah's birth God has not spoken to me in anything resembling consciously apprehended words. He has, however, spoken through dreams and coincidences too synchronous to be accidental. I have been made aware of his infinite power, and I give thanks every day that such omnipotence is tempered by absolute love. As a father, son, brother, friend, I have been grievously angered by those closest to me. Within our family, brother has betrayed brother, father daughter, mother son, and on and on into the infinity of miseries we impose best upon those we love. That misery at times may become unbearable. I have held a brother trembling at gunpoint, have hunted another with the firm intention of killing him. God pulled me back or directed me away each of those times. It is my belief that God must have difficulty staying his own hand so often is he insulted, abused, or worse, imperiously dismissed. An ancient symbol, the Sword of Damocles, is an appropriate and classical metaphor for our human condition relative to God. I have felt His power, been visited by His Spirit, and am able to attest: The brutal instrument threatening to bring to life the final moment of our reality hangs close above our heads. Fortunately, the sword of God is hung by no slender thread of hair, and it is ever stayed in its downward sweep by a Father's irrational love for his children. We all shall die, but God will not destroy or even harm us.

A more modern metaphor is to be found in Pynchon's *Gravity's Rainbow*. In this modern age the missile has been launched and has reached its apogee. Upon us all and perhaps upon all our kind obliteration descends. We sit in our own cave of shadows, our *cinema*, blissfully existing in our insubstantial reality while the natural force of our own gravity draws death down upon us. That the instrument of our demise may be manned by a sex-slave teenager and launched by a madman is not the work of God. It is of our own creation, and we live and die in our own land. Many of us have sought more or at least other. Many such as I, not of the preterite although it is with them that my heart dwells, have been somehow elected to know God and to, in our own inadequate human ways, share that knowledge with anyone who might listen. In that light and with that purpose I launch the final chapter of this narrative and of my life.

I SPECIFICALLY REFER to the ICBM above my own head, Cancer. I also, once again, find George to be a most important player in my personal drama. God too, of course, but this time he spoke not a word.

To begin, George is, to my mind but not to his own, obsessive concerning his health and his prospects for a long life. In light of these concerns, when he turned fifty he embarked upon the first of several explorations of his digestive system, a sigmoidoscopy. One morning over coffee he asserted that I too should avail myself of the procedure, "A must for anyone over fifty," he perkily asserted. "I just had one, and I'm as fit as you can get."

The hell with that I thought. I'd rather not know early on if I have cancer. It seemed better to be surprised just before the scythe swung my way than to spend years cowering before its imagined sweep. I continued on my blissful way. Despite my knowledge to the contrary, I felt assured of my immunity to diseases such as cancer. Like my father I would die of a heart attack or like my cousin—even better—possessed of wind and speed, suddenly cut free from the tug of gravity, the oppression of mortal life. So I thought. I would live a shooting star, not a feeble old man with a tube stuck up his ass. Really!

George can be just a trifle annoying about some things, and this was one of them. A direct result of his obsessive promptings, I investigated colon cancer and the related procedures, and among my discoveries was the fact (The very latest research to some degree questions this) that colonoscopies, not sigmoidoscopies, are the gold standard for accurate prevention as well as diagnosis. This information I gleefully shared with my friend who, true to his obsessive nature, immediately said he would take the issue up with his doctor. So much for my triumph. Foiled again.

As far as I knew I had only one significant health concern. Ever since adulthood I had been subject to periodic attacks of prostatitis. For years I would hold off going to a doctor until the pain became unbearable and my urine contained more pus than water. For a long time I patronized one urologist who tolerated my alcoholic and overall careless as well as clueless habits. Eventually he retired, but I found another even more willing to treat me on an as-needed basis. No PSA, not even the dreaded rectal. Just the Cipro. Then he disappeared into a haze of allegations and accusations leaving me with naught but the Emergency Department of Samaritan Hospital as my specialist of choice.

The situations I found myself in there were not always grim. I got to know one of the ED nurses and much of the staff. We always had as much fun at my expense as we could dredge up from the circumstances. And since those circumstances were usually pretty extreme I rarely had to suffer the indignity of the rectal exam. Always the doctor would refer me to a urologist. Always I refused.

Into this ongoing set of events seeped George's warning hard upon the discovery of a possible flaw in my overall immunity to serious disease. One morning after a particularly long run—ten or twelve miles—and fast, for me anyway—7:15 pace—I had an attack of bloody diarrhea, and then about a month later, after a shorter, faster run, the same. However, I warded off further attacks by keeping my pace no faster than eight-minute miles. I bled no more. But the bloody seed had been planted. Did I have that which my research suggested, diverticulosis/itis, or was it something worse? Cancer.

And, of course, inescapable as my own mortality, George ran ever at my side; his mouth ran ever into my ear. Colonoscopy.

No way. But then one day, as I wiped myself after a BM a fleck of blood, small but unmistakable, appeared upon my morning paper. I could not help myself, I wiped again. More blood. Gently I probed the offending area, and there swelled a lump of some strange tissue. A tumor? A polyp? A hemorrhoid my research suggested. It did only offer blood sporadically and only after the most vigorous exercises of my excretory functions and responses. I knew it was nothing or at least not much. But then I felt afraid.

I prayed to God to take my affliction away. He did not. Tormented by doubt and fear, allowing myself to forget most of the lessons I had learned throughout my life, for a time I became obsessed by perhaps the lowest of my human functions. I soon became a fool even in my own eyes. I would rather die than be a fool, especially a self-aware fool, and so I sought a way out. An appointment with a gastroenterologist might have been my best option, but then, remember, I was dealing with James Slattery, a self-acknowledged fool.

Did this fool's solution spring from within his often fertile imagination or did God answer my prayer in his own often indirect way? I do not know. I don't and didn't care. I established a plan of action which I pledged to myself I would follow no matter what. The best part of the plan was that it did not involve a colonoscopy.

My plan, perhaps proposal would be a more accurate term,

involved a deal between myself and, who else, God. I would proceed with my life as though all were well, only submitting to medical impositions if the following events were to occur: First, If I were to have another prostate infection—it had been two years and I had convinced myself that phase of my dance with ill-health had ended—I would go to the emergency room, and if they didn't do a rectal exam then, I would heed their suggestions and follow up with a urologist. Ah, blissful ignorance. Not six weeks after my foolish pledge I felt the familiar fire down below. I held off as long as I could until I could stand it no longer and visited Samaritan's ED. The doctor did no rectal, but did offer a referral to Dr. C, a Troy urologist. I delayed, but in a few weeks reluctantly called for an appointment. And thereafter came the shock.

My urine showed no infection. But, upon completion of the prostate massage, the doctor turned and spoke in somewhat somber tones, "Your prostate seems fine. But you have blood in your stool." Dr. C, as far as he was aware, was the only urologist routinely doing a guaiac on all his patients. He had found that which I had wished would remain hidden. From Dr. C I went to Dr. B who scheduled a colonoscopy. The colonoscopy found, and the doctor excised a huge adenoma (precancerous polyp) as well as one other less ominous adenoma and two of the benign sort. As he said in my follow-up visit after the tests had come back negative, "You're lucky." Yes, Dr. B, yourself I am certain a man who was no stranger to God, I was lucky, but not in the usual sense. My luck was and is that God, for his own as yet mysterious reasons, cares enough to shepherd this fool through this life despite the idiot's best efforts to stray over some precipice or other.

And that was not enough. Until my first visit to Dr. C, I had not had a PSA. He changed all that. My first was so normal as to be almost boring. At the time he gave me the results, I had, as he stated, "bigger fish to fry," since my adenoma had been detected but the biopsy results not in. So thank you, God, Dr. C, and Dr. B for saving my life.

But not so fast. The very next year, my PSA, while still in the normal range had doubled, and Dr. C did a biopsy. Six of the seven samples were benign. But, oh that seventh! I had prostate cancer.

Originally, the prognosis was good. The operation told a slightly more discouraging story. The actual tumor was higher on the Gleason scale than the biopsy had shown, and the tumor had reached the margin of the gland, leaving me with a 50/50 probability of the cancer having spread to surrounding tissue. God's mercy had brought me here. Not to certainty. Not to good health. Not to rejuvenation. God had thrust me directly back into my father's car. The approaching specter was no beat up family sedan. I was racing headlong into death by cancer.

THE NEXT MORNING after hearing the fatal news, an old and beaten man sits at his kitchen table. His wife and children are not at home. He has not shared his grim prospects with them. He will not. His doctor has assured him that the next step, should the cancer return—if it has never really gone away—would be radiation, and that would in all likelihood resolve the problem. The old man will do as fate dictates, but he knows. He is dead and merely waiting to be so declared.

The mailman stops outside and leaves the mail. Even dead, the old man will not fade easily into the darkness he has already entered. He has, despite the doctor's explicit orders, already done his ten sets of stairs. He will walk to curbside and retrieve his mail as well. Dylan Thomas thunders within the echo chambers of his frozen brain. He will not go gentle. His cane pounds the asphalt of the drive. His throat gravels an animal's warning. *Rage! Rage!* And he begins to feel alive.

The trouble with rage is that it is hard to sustain. It needs release, and, when none is forthcoming, it quickly fades to gloom. And so.... Once again the old man sits at his kitchen table despair in his heart and the sharp bite of Nothing tearing at his soul. Bills, bills, nothing but goddamn bills. But nestled amid the notices of payment due rests a blue envelope addressed to Mr. James Slattery, no return address. Just his luck, he supposes, some student or group of them thinks he has taken leave for something trivial and has sent him some mildly offensive, humorous sick card. But, he would have done the same thing.

Inside is a beautiful cream and violet card of luxurious stock. A picture of the Most Holy mother stands out from her surroundings, a smile of love and a pose of elegant compassion. Inside, within a flowered border and beneath a bedecked cross, no longer the death of Jesus, but rather the symbol of his life, is the message. It is a mass card of sorts. An order of priests in the mid-west will offer a week's sequence of masses for him, and he will be in their prayers for a full year. It is signed simply: Tracy Daley.

Tracy Daley is a student in a computer-centered composition class of his. The old man, even when young, had always believed certain people had spirits or souls which were compatible from before their human manifestations and which linked these people in some inexpressible and infinite way. Upon their first meeting, he had felt that way about Tracy, and as they grew to know each other, had understood that they were brother and sister, that a compassion and love existed between them which defied understanding, and yet they both understood.

I PRESSED THE card to my cheek, held it to my quiet heart. God had sent me Tracy Daley, and Tracy Daley had sent the card. The card spoke for God, not as before in thunderous command, but gently, soft as a woman's eyes when she looks upon her child. All would go as God intended. I would live to find more beauty and joy than I could imagine; and I would die in love and beauty despite my rage. I would need to go gentle into my own good night, much as I, so very long ago, would have that afternoon on the Pennsylvania highway. I still rage, but I do not fear. I will fight unto my last breath, but not for life.

I will fight the natural human urge to survive at all costs. I will forbid it in my family's vision of my last days. No one puts up a valiant fight against the diseases like cancer, end-stage renal disease, and Alzheimer's which afflict us at the end. I have read too many times how some newly dead human has waged "courageous battle" against these scourges. Remember. When the terminal disease strikes, you must endure it. When you know there is no hope of victory, there is no courageous resistance. The one facing termination has but three choices.

Choice one is the classic existential freedom I have faced ever since becoming both self-aware and enlightened by Camus' *The Myth of Sisyphus*. Suicide. I have lived with that option since my first recognition that I was condemned to die. I have always rejected it. I have not chosen it in the face of death and neither will I opt for an easy way out of despair and Ivan Ilych pain. What I may decide if faced with Alzheimer's or some other form of developing dementia, I do not at this time know. If God remains merciful, I will not have to find out.

Choice two is prolonging life at all costs. That, as indicated above, is no option for me. Again, as I have stated previously, I have no fear of death. I can imagine a time when he might even become a hoped for visitor to my bedside. I may, as Alla often did, call out for him at moments of weakness. How great must the fear of Death be to someone who prefers insane hope curdled by excruciating pain to death, even if that death truly is the end, and all ends badly even for those who have lived well? My own logic, given these perceptions and unanswerable questions, concludes that rather than being a courageous struggle, the extended treatment and insistence upon heroic medical interventions are the result of a dread so overpowering that the word "fear" does it no justice.

Caesar speaks, "Cowards die many times before their deaths. / The valiant never taste of death but once." I first read the play in ninth-grade English. We read it aloud, each student given a chance at Shakespeare. As luck or fate might have it, I was assigned Caesar, and I read his lines to Susan W's Calpurnia. From the beginning I took them to heart; I would die but once, when my time came, and fear not until that appointed hour. As is perhaps painfully obvious to anyone who knows me, I have always been attracted to the dark and dramatic.

But then, even more painfully obvious, at least to me, is the fact that I have faced death on more than one occasion, and have tasted his not always bitter brew perhaps too many times. Am I then, by Caesar's definition, not a Coward? A college Shakespeare class suggested an answer. By the time I went to college I had more than once died, at least by my own reckoning, and those experiences had empowered me, not weakened me. My class explained how that could still be tragic, heroic, and Shakespearian. The poet's coward's death is fear. The coward loses all nobility as a result of that fear, for, rather than facing and conquering his enemy, he submits and acts accordingly. At all costs, he avoids death, the object of his abject terror. Now, I do not claim to be valiant. In fact, to Aristotle, who saw fit to ascribe courage exclusively to virtuous and aware men who faced death on the battlefield, neither the wild lion, a symbol of courage for many, nor the equally unafraid Celt is courageous. Lack of fear, such as is the state of the beast and this modern-day descendent of the ancient warriors, precludes courage. True courage, that which the valiant possess, results from conquering fear, not freedom from it. Therefore, I am not valiant; I simply have no fear. At least of death.

The final choice is to be aware. To love the life and the people in it that you are about to leave, and to be strong. To maintain your dignity, and, in your own non-Aristotelian manner, to have courage. Let no one hear your cries. Show no one, especially those you love, the face of your pain. And tell them, each and every one of them, that you love them. My hope is that I may succeed in this particular nobility that can spring from dying well.

If I succeed, I owe it to Leo Tolstoy, to Tracy Daley, to Michael, to my parents, to my children, to Pam, and to God. Through them I have learned how best to die, which is a simple yet necessary part of learning to live a complete and worthwhile life. They have made me strong. And, finally, because of them and others as well, I have learned to care.

Caring for all things and all people, for my own self as well, is most basically the true and actual meaning of life, as many before me have understood, and its source is clear. Earlier in this essay I wrote, "This piece is...the expression of a developing awareness—knowledge and understanding—of something which may be termed Spirit or God as well as other names too numerous to mention," and expressed a cautious optimism that I might by the end have achieved the understanding I lacked even so short a time ago as last month when I first began to write. As I had hoped, the chronicling of these experiences has focused my thoughts. And the answer is neither blowing in the wind nor is it of such esoteric nature as to be understood only by philosophers and their like. The answer has been right before my eyes in some form or other since I first noticed a Bible.

Jesus spoke many truths. One truth most Christians would like to ignore is that He spoke to all of humankind. He would not condemn the atheist or the Taoist any more than he condemned the "Woman taken in adultery," or even those who crucified Him. His words are for the World in spite of its multitude of sectarian beliefs. One need not be a physicist to accept Newton's Law of Gravity nor a chemist to accept that matter may occur in three states, solid, liquid or gas. The same with the truth as spoken by anyone: the Prophet Mohammed, Moses, Lao Tsu...or Jesus. My personal choice for the ultimate satisfaction of my quest for value and meaning in the face of death, perhaps coincidentally due to my origins as Irish-American and Roman Catholic, is the wisdom of the man called Jesus, but I do not think the particular teachings to which I refer should ring untrue in any thinking person's ears.

I quote Matthew 22:37-39: "Love the Lord your God with all your heart and with all your soul and with all your mind. This is the first and greatest commandment. And the second is like it: Love your neighbor as yourself." In simpler terms: Love God and love each other. That is enough. And so, at the end of my life's journey, after all has been done and undone, achieved and sacrificed, I come to the awareness that those words have always been with me, but for most of my life I have sought more, as did Tolstoy. The tortured writer first turned to the "simple faith" of the peasants, but he, as scholar and intellectual, quickly found himself unable to accept such as an answer to his questions concerning the meaning and purpose of existence. The simple is so profoundly inadequate to the task of satisfying the inquiring mind that the intellectual is compelled to seek complexity before once again resolving everything back into simplicity. Such is the paradox of understanding: The necessary way to the simplest of truths often requires an embrace of and subsequent rejection of the multiple facets of deception. In another expression of a related nature, the straight and narrow path to awareness is often intricately knotted about itself and infinitely open to seductive digressions.

At the end, Ivan Ilych rejects all the illusions he has built up around himself and discovers the bold radiance of truth. But this became possible only after he felt his son's tears and was moved to repent of the life he had lived. Not until that point when he "actually" began to care for those about him did "He whose understanding mattered" understand. Only then could Ivan see that, "In place of death there [is] light"[11] We, every bit as much as Ivan, can find this truth, immortal in the face of death. Even should we wait until the very end to discover it, if only we will follow the sometimes not so simple path of love for each other and for God, despite the twists and turnings of our lives, we will find not mere pleasure and mortal happiness.

We will discover Joy.

NOTES

1 Castaneda, p 27.

2 Tolstoy, p 1270.

3 Stills, 1982.

4 Tolstoy, *The Death of Ivan Ilych.* p 1304.

5 *Ibid.* p 1303.

6 Einstein, 1955.

7 Mc Broom, 1977.

8 Unamuno, p 120.

9 Alcoholics Anonymous.

10 Unamuno, p 120.

11. Tolstoy, *The Death of Ivan Ilych.* p 1304.

James J. Slattery

Selected Bibliography

Camus, Alfred (1983). *The Myth of Sisyphus and Other Essays* (J. O'brien, Trans.). New York: Vintage Books. (1942).

Castaneda, Carlos (1996). *The Teachings of Don Juan: A Yaqui Way of Knowledge.* Berkeley: University of California Press.

Castaneda, Carlos (1992). *Tales of Power.* New York: Washington Square Press.

De Unamuno, Miguel (1912). *Tragic Sense of Life* (J.E.C. Flitch Trans.). New York: Dover Publications.

Dostoevsky, Fyodor (1996). *The Brothers Karamazov* (C. Garnett, Trans.). New York: The Modern Library. (1879-80).

Dylan, Bob (1988). Death is not the End. On *Down in the Groove.* U.S.: Columbia Records.

Einstein, Albert (1955). Letter to the family of Michelangelo Besso. Retrieved from http://www.brainathlete.com/closest-friendships-albert-einstein/.

Eliot, T. S. (1963). *Collected Poems.* New York: Harcourt Brace & Company.

Hopkins, Gerard Manley (1918). *Poems.* London: Humphrey Milford.

Hunter, Robert (1971. Ripple [Recorded by the Grateful Dead]. On *American Beauty.* U.S.: Warner Bros. Records.

Kumar, Manjit (2008). *Quantum.* New York: W. W. Norton & Company.

Lao Tsu (5th Century BCE). *Tao Te Ching.*

Mc Broom, Amanda (1977). Retrieved from http://www.amcbroom.com/rose.html.

Nagel, Thomas (2012). *Mind & Cosmos.* New York: Oxford

University Press.

Nietzsche, Friedrich (2005). *Thus Spoke Zarathustra* (C. Martin Trans). New York: Barnes & Noble Classics.

Pynchon, Thomas (1973). *Gravity's Rainbow.* New York: Viking Press.

Rosenblum, B and Kuttner, F. (2011). *Quantum Enigma.* New York: Oxford University Press.

Ruprecht, Louis A. (2008). *The Tragic Gospel: How John Corrupted the Heart of Christianity.* San Francisco: Jossey-Bass.

Shakespeare, William (1914). *The Oxford Shakespeare.* London: Oxford University Press.

Stills, Stephen (1982). Southern Cross. On *Daylight Again.* New York: Atlantic.

Tolstoy, Leo (1886). *The Death of Ivan Ilych* (L. Maude and A. Maude Trans.).

Tolstoy, Leo (1899). *The Gospel in Brief.* (Isabel Hapsgood Trans.).

Tolstoy, Leo (1894) *The Kingdom of God is Within You* (C. Garnett Trans.).

Tolstoy, Leo (1886). *What I Believe* (C. Popov Trans.).

ABOUT THE AUTHOR

James J. Slattery is a teacher, a husband, father and friend. He is a recovering alcoholic, a born-again Christian who considers himself a Catholic, and something of an enigma even to himself. He has written DIE LIVE LOVE in hope that it will offer some glimmer of their own possibilities to those fallen into any of the various black holes similar to his own.

Once he scorned the Beatles' lyric, "All you need is love." Now he finds it profound.

James J. Slattery

DIE LIVE LOVE

* 9 7 8 0 6 9 2 2 6 5 3 7 6 *